THE SMALL MEMBERSHIP CHURCH
SCENARIOS FOR TOMORROW

Ministry for the Third Millennium

THE SMALL MEMBERSHIP CHURCH

Scenarios for Tomorrow

LYLE E. SCHALLER

ABINGDON PRESS / Nashville

THE SMALL MEMBERSHIP CHURCH
SCENARIOS FOR TOMORROW

Copyright © 1994 by Abingdon Press

This book is printed on recycled, acid-free paper.

Library of Congress Cataloging-in-Publication Data

Schaller, Lyle E.
    The small membership church: scenarios for tomorrow/Lyle E. Schaller.
        p.   cm.—(Ministry for the third millennium)
    ISBN 0-687-38718-3 (pbk.: alk. paper)
    1. Small churches.   2. Christianity—Forecasting.   I. Title.
II. Series.
BV637.8.S34   1994
254—dc20   94-19623
                                                                                                          CIP

94 95 96 97 98 99 00 01 02 03 — 10 9 8 7 6 5 4 3 2 1

MANUFACTURED IN THE UNITED STATES OF AMERICA

To
Kenneth H. Sauer
and
Andrew J. White

CONTENTS

INTRODUCTION

For many observers of the world scene, the fall of the Berlin Wall in November 1989 came as a tremendous shock. At least a few reacted by defining that event as the end of the twentieth century. An even greater shock came on September 13, 1993, when two longtime enemies, Yitzhak Rabin and Yasser Arafat, stood in front of the White House and shook hands.[1]

Why were these two events among the greatest news stories of the twentieth century? One reason is that each marked the end of an era. A second is that the widely held assumptions of a few years earlier made both events appear to be highly unlikely elements of the future.

This book is organized around three theses. The first is that, for nearly four centuries, the small congregation has been the dominant institutional expression of Protestant Christianity on the North American continent.

The second thesis is that the societal context for the small Protestant church has changed from supportive to neutral to, in many places, a hostile environment. The small Protestant congregation once thrived in a society dominated by small social institutions, most of which were friendly toward and supportive of the churches. Today the small church exists in a culture dominated by large institutions, most of which do not make any effort to be supportive of organized religion.[2]

One example is the retailer who never opened his store before noon on Sunday. Today many retailers are eager to welcome customers two or three hours before noon or earlier on Sunday. A second is municipal governments, county governments, and local boards of education that once were eager to cooperate with the churches. Today not only is that rare, but also municipal officials are becoming increasingly reluctant to issue building permits for the use of land for religious purposes.[3]

The third thesis is that small churches have a bright and promising future—if they are willing to adapt to a new role in a changing culture. That is the theme of the fifth chapter, which identifies a list of 44 alternative courses of action for the leaders in small churches. That, however, is not the place to begin this discussion. A better beginning point is to review some of the assumptions on which those three theses are based.[4] While far from being an exhaustive list, these assumptions do help to explain why others may arrive at a different set of conclusions about the role of the small church in the third millennium.

1. The small church is not a miniature version of the large congregation. The small congregation is to the megachurch what the village is to the large central city. They are different orders of God's creation. (See chapter 1.)

2. The small church naturally tends to be the dominant institutional expression of Protestant Christianity on the North American continent. The natural and predictable tendency is

(a) for Protestant churches to be small and (b) for larger congregations to shrink in size as the decades roll past.

3. In the year 2020, congregations averaging fewer than a hundred at worship will represent at least 40 percent of all the Protestant churches in the United States and Canada—and that proportion may be closer to 50 percent. In those denominations with a strong pro-small congregation orientation and a powerful anti-large church bias, that proportion may exceed 70 percent in 2020.

4. A growing proportion of small congregations will depend on bivocational pastors and bivocational ministerial teams, rather than on a full-time and fully credentialed resident pastor for ministerial leadership.

5. On the list of the most attractive alternatives for the small church looking forward to the twenty-first century, merger with another small congregation should rank no higher than 42 and disbanding or closing or dissolving should rank no higher than 44. (See chapter 5.)

6. Numerical growth should never be the top priority for the small church that has been in existence for a decade or longer. If substantial numerical growth does appear to be both possible and desirable, that should not be perceived as the number-one priority. In those situations, the number-one priority should be planned change initiated from within the organization. The heart of the issue is planned change, not simply numerical growth. The central assumption is that small churches cannot enjoy substantial numerical growth without making what many will identify as unwelcome or disruptive changes.[5]

7. If the goal is numerical growth, the leaders should accept that they will be competing with other congregations for prospective new members. Intercongregational cooperation on ministry and programing such as worship, music, Christian education, and pastoral care may be compatible with shrinking in numbers or perhaps in remaining on a plateau in size, but it is

not compatible with a strategy for numerical growth. (See chapter 3.)

8. Effective pastoral service in a small church requires a different set of gifts, skills, priorities, and personal characteristics than are required to be the effective senior pastor of a large congregation.

9. The most influential criteria for evaluating staff in the small church often include (a) skills in interpersonal relationships, (b) depth of a personal Christian commitment, (c) instant availability, and (d) a willingness to focus on the parishioners' agenda. In the large church, the basic criteria are more likely to include (a) professional competence, (b) leadership ability, and (c) effectiveness in completing an assignment with better-than-expected results.

10. A decreasing proportion of regular churchgoers display a preference, if circumstances offer them a range of choices, for the small church. Those who prefer the small church tend to come in disproportionately large numbers from among (a) people born before 1940, (b) those who place relationships above the quality of ministry, (c) adults on the liberal end of the theological spectrum, (d) seminary-trained clergy who graduated in a class that included fewer than one hundred candidates for the M.Div. degree, and (e) adults who spent their formative years in a small church in small-town or rural communities.

11. In several traditions, defenders of the small church build a strong ideological argument that small is good and big is bad. This argument often is used to explain why large congregations should provide financial subsidies for small churches.

12. Long-established large congregations tend to be fragile institutions, while small churches tend to be institutionally hardy and tough.

13. The smaller the congregation, the more influential are the volunteer lay leaders in formulating policies. The larger the

congregation, the more influential are the senior minister and the paid program staff in making policy.

14. Participatory democracy is an appropriate system of governance in the small church, while the middle-sized congregation naturally chooses a representative system of church government. In the large churches, a higher premium often is placed on competence, commitment, experience, and performance. One common result in very large congregations is governance by an elite group. A second is that as the number of members goes up, the size of the governing board goes down. A third is a greater dependence on standing committees in smaller congregations and greater use of task forces and ad hoc committees in large churches.

15. Given the limitations on discretionary resources (such as the time and energy of volunteers or money), the governing board in the small church often perceives itself as a rationing or permission-giving and permission-withholding body. By contrast, the governing board in the large church is more likely to see itself as a long-range planning group responsible for inventing a new tomorrow.

16. Continuity in the large churches tends to be in the senior minister, the staff, the ministries and program, and a distinctive identity. In small congregations, the central threads of continuity tend to be in (a) local traditions; (b) real estate; (c) the racial, nationality, language, or ethnic heritage; (d) kinship and friendship ties; (e) the relationships among the people; and (f) volunteer leaders.

17. A change in pastors is more likely to be a disruptive incident in the large congregation than in the small church. (See points 12-16 above.)

18. That dependence on lay leadership can justify short pastorates of four to seven years in the small churches, while the ideal pastorate in a large congregation will be fifteen to forty years.

19. The smaller the number of members, the more likely the focus in program planning will be on Sunday. The larger the congregation, the more likely worship, the teaching ministries, the nurturing of the group life, and the creation of attractive entry points for first-time visitors will be scattered through the week.[6]

20. In the small congregation, the Sunday morning schedule and program usually are designed with the members as the number-one constituency. In larger and numerically growing churches, it is more likely that the primary constituency for planning Sunday morning will be first-time visitors.

21. The limitations on discretionary resources often means the small church can offer people only two choices: "Take it or leave it." By contrast, many large congregations are able to offer people a broader range of attractive experiences in worship, in the teaching ministry, in music, in fellowship opportunities, in personal involvement in missions, in youth programming, and in the group life of that parish.

22. Good blood lines, a body temperature between 98° and 99° (F), a willingness to serve, and friendship ties are among the most influential factors in the selection and placement of volunteers in many small churches. In most large congregations, skill, completion of a training experience, vision, a powerful future orientation, a willingness to serve, and Christian commitment are among the most influential factors in the selection and placement of volunteers.

23. The focus on the members, the importance of interpersonal relationships, and the benefits of volunteer participation support strong lay leadership in Sunday morning worship in the small church.

By contrast, the focus on first-time visitors, the emphasis on quality, and the need to speak to the religious needs of people (see chapter 1) suggest Laity Sunday (sometimes called "Amateur Hour") is an appropriate event on the annual calendar in the small congregation, but not in the big church.

24. It may be appropriate for the pastor of the small congregation to reprimand the members during Sunday morning worship. That is not appropriate behavior in any congregation that hopes first-time visitors will return next week.

25. The smaller the number of members, the lower the annual turnover rate in the membership. The small church usually must replace 3 to 6 percent of the members annually to remain on a plateau in size. The large church often must replace 8 to 20 percent annually to remain on a plateau in size.

26. Large and middle-sized congregations usually are either growing or shrinking in numbers, while small churches often find it relatively easy to remain on a plateau in size for decades.

27. The financial needs of the institution often become the number-one motivating force behind second-mile giving by the members of the small church. The primary motivation for second-mile giving by members of the large congregation often is (a) missions and outreach and/or (b) the vision of a new tomorrow and the challenge to turn that vision into reality.

28. If and when the circumstances call for two weekend worship services in the small church, they are likely to be carbon copies, while in the large congregation they are more likely to be designed as two different worship experiences for two different constituencies.

29. The larger the number of members, the larger the number of dollars per worshiper that will be required to pay all the bills. In 1995, many small congregations could pay all of their bills on time if the weekly offering was equivalent to $7 to $15 times the worship attendance. In large congregations, that figure was more likely to be $15 to $35 times the worship attendance.

30. In smaller congregations, Sunday school often is the heart of the teaching ministry. In larger churches, the Sunday school may rank third or fourth or fifth in importance in the teaching ministry behind (a) the sermon, (b) evening Bible study groups,

(c) daytime study groups, or (d) educational trips of five to fifteen days.

31. The larger the size of the congregation, the longer the time frame needed for planning. In many small congregations, the time frame for planning is two to six months. In very large churches, it often is two to ten years.

32. A central theme in the life of the small church is the life cycle of the individual—birth, baptism, confirmation, marriage, birth of a baby, retirement, death of a spouse, and the death of that member. In the larger congregations, the central theme may be the spiritual or faith journey of the individual from inquirer or searcher or seeker to believer to disciple to volunteer minister.

33. For many small congregations, the denominational affiliation continues to be an important part of self-identification. The larger the number of members, the less influential is the denominational label in terms of self-identification.

34. The small church usually perceives Sunday morning to be the number-one entry point for newcomers. The large church defines Sunday morning as only one of several attractive entry points for first-time visitors.

35. The smaller the number of members, the smaller the proportion of total expenditures allocated to advertising. The larger the number of members and/or the greater the desire to reach new generations, the larger the amount of money spent on public relations.

36. If it does advertise in the local newspaper, the small congregation is likely to rely on the "tombstone" ad that carries the name of the church, the name of the pastor, the address, the denominational affiliation, and the Sunday schedule. The large congregation is more likely to focus on the needs of the reader in designing that newspaper advertisement. (See chapter 4.)

37. The grapevine often is one of the two or three most valuable channels of internal communication in the small

church. In the large congregation, the grapevine often does more harm than good.

38. The small congregation rarely receives a newcomer who was first attracted to that congregation by television. It is not unusual for very large churches to report that close to one-half of their new members came in response to a television program or commercial featuring that congregation.

39. For instrumental music support for worship, the small church is more likely to rely on a piano or an electronic organ or a sound system with recorded music, while the large congregation is more likely to utilize a pipe organ or an orchestra or a band or a team of seven to twenty worship leaders.

40. In the small church, the primary institutional loyalty of the individual often is to that congregation. In the large congregation, the primary institutional loyalty of many individuals is to a choir, a Sunday school class, the youth group, a circle in the women's organization, an adult study group, a band or orchestra, a program committee, a mutual support group, or a small Bible study and prayer cell.

41. In identifying prospective future members, the small congregation usually begins by focusing on (a) kinfolk of members, (b) friends and neighbors of members, and (c) people without any active church involvement who live within a mile or two of that congregation's meeting place.

By contrast, most large and rapidly growing churches think in regional, not neighborhood, terms and focus more on people's spiritual and personal needs rather than on established kin or friendship ties or place of residence or geographical proximity.

42. In the small church, the term "ministry of music" usually is a synonym for one to four choirs, plus two or three volunteer leaders. In the large church, the ministry of music often includes five to twenty music groups and three or more paid staff members.

43. In most small churches, the number-one reference point when the discussion turns to "quality" is the quality of interper-

sonal relationships among the members. A close number two is the quality of the match between the pastor and the parishioners.

By contrast, in the large congregation, discussions on "quality" tend to focus on the quality and relevance of the preaching, on the worship experiences, on the teaching ministry, on pastoral care, on administration, and on the real estate.

44. Finally, the most important assumption on which this book is based can be expressed in three words: **Churches can change!** As the context for congregational life changes, as older members disappear from the scene, and as new generations come along, churches can change. As many of the assumptions identified here suggest, change is more difficult in smaller congregations than it is in big churches.

While it is far from exhaustive, this long list of assumptions is offered here for three reasons. First, these assumptions constitute the foundation for most of what is discussed in subsequent pages. Any disagreement the reader may have with a specific diagnostic or prescriptive comment may be based on a difference between the assumptions carried by the reader with the assumptions carried by this author. This is not a value-free or neutral book!

Second, these assumptions help to explain why small congregations are not miniature versions of large churches and why large churches are not enlarged versions of small congregations. They are different orders of creation. They function around different sets of central organizing principles. What is an appropriate leadership model for a minister in one often will be inappropriate in the other. The appropriate priorities for the small church rarely are the appropriate priorities for the large congregation.

Finally, and perhaps most important for the reader of this book, these assumptions help to explain why the operational response to God's call to be faithful and obedient will not be the same in the twenty-first century for the small church as the operational response of the large parish. They enter into their journey into the third millennium from different beginning points, and they do not share a common destination.

The world is filled with people who seek simple answers to complex issues. One example is the scribe who challenged Jesus to identify the greatest commandment of all. Jesus answered that there are two (Mark 12:28-31). These two commandments also offer a conceptual framework for identifying the basic differences between the best of the small congregations and the best of the large churches. That is the central theme of the first chapter of this book.

The second chapter documents the fact that the small church is the normative institutional expression of Protestant Christianity on the North American continent.

During the first half of the twentieth century, the ideologically correct stance of mainline Protestant leaders was to encourage intercongregational and interdenominational cooperation. The widespread ownership of the private automobile, including ownership by hundreds of thousands of teenagers, plus other changes described in this book mean that the vast majority of small churches today are competing with other congregations for future generations of members. The meeting place of some of these competing churches may be as far as ten to twenty miles away. What is the appropriate stance of today's small churches? To encourage intercongregational cooperation in programming or to recognize that competition is the new fact of life? That conflict is the subject of the third chapter.

One beginning point for the leaders in the small church as they plan for the twenty-first century is to seek to perpetuate yesterday as much as possible. A second is to recognize that most congregations are really confronted with two choices: change or gradually fade away. An introduction to this discussion is the theme of the fourth chapter.

A different beginning point is to review specific courses of action. A total of 44 are presented in the fifth chapter, in the format of six categories with the most promising discussed first and the least promising last.

Finally, a brief chapter summarizes some of the crucial learnings about the identity, role, and central characteristics of today's small churches.

This book is a product of working with a variety of small churches over the past four decades. It is dedicated to two long-time friends. Unfortunately, it is impossible to identify and list all the other individuals to whom I am also indebted for their comments, criticisms, ideas, insights, reflections, and wisdom, but that debt must be acknowledged at least in general terms. Thank you all!

1.

THE SECOND GREAT COMMANDMENT

I n "The Death of the Hired Man," one of his earliest and best-known poems, Robert Frost recounts the story of Silas, the hired man, who returns to live with Warren and Mary. Earlier, at the close of the haying season the previous summer, Warren had warned Silas that if he left at that busy time of the season, he should not return. One day when Warren was away, Silas comes back. Later, when Warren returns, Mary tells him that Silas has come home to die. Warren wonders why Silas doesn't go to live with his well-to-do brother, who is a director of the bank, "a somebody" who lives only thirteen miles away. Mary explains why Silas has come to them to find a place to die.

> "Home is the place where, when you have to go there,
> They have to take you in."

A half century later, ex-President Lyndon B. Johnson expanded on that definition by adding that home is a place where they take care of you when you are ill and they mourn when you die.

Those also are three of the central characteristics of one model of the small church. That model resembles an extended family. In addition to proclaiming the gospel of Jesus Christ and administering the sacraments, these small churches also take you in without question when you return from a long absence, they care for you when you are ill, and they mourn when you die.

Two simple riddles help to explain the nature of these congregations—and also serve to introduce two models of healthy small churches. First, in 1990 the proportion of mature adults, age sixty-five and over, residing in Florida was 45 percent above the figure for the United States, but the death rate in Florida in 1990 was only 21 percent above the death rate for the nation. Why?

One part of the answer is that the census of population counts people where they are residing on April 1, and some of the "Snowbirds" do not return north until late April or May. Second, mature Northerners in very poor health are less likely to relocate to the Sunbelt than are their peers who enjoy good health. Third, and more to the point, a substantial number of retirees, when they realize death is coming closer, go back home to spend their last days with kinfolk and friends. They go home to die. This pattern is most common among those who have experienced the death of a spouse.

Those who return to a very large church up North where they were members are surprised, overwhelmed, perhaps even intimidated by so many of the strange faces they encounter. "It seems like half of the people we saw on our first Sunday back must have joined since we left nine years ago."

In many large congregations the real proportion may be closer to 70 percent rather than only half. A fortunate few return first to that adult Sunday school class that they helped to pioneer three decades earlier and where they were pillars for twenty years.

Three-quarters of the current class are old friends, and they sincerely and eagerly ask about "John" or "Martha" or mourn the death of "Harold."

Those who move "back home" after a five- or ten-year absence and return to that small church filled with kinfolk and friends from earlier days often are welcomed home as though they had never left. "Don't tell me it's been ten years! It seems like you've only been gone a few weeks." "My! You haven't changed a bit!" (And neither have we.)

Like a good Christian home, these small churches welcome back former members without question or reservation. That welcome also extends, incidentally, to the pastor who left twenty-five years ago and has come "back home" for retirement or to be buried in the local cemetery.

These small churches act out Robert Frost's statement that "home is the place where they have to take you in."

The "Cheers" Model

A second riddle questions the popularity of the television program "Cheers." Why was this situation comedy so popular back in the late 1980s and early 1990s? What does its theme song say to the distinctive identity of many small churches? Why was this the most-watched television program of its era? One reason was that people identified with it. That small tavern is a place where "everybody is glad you came," the regulars have a right to be there. They are expected to drop in.

Second, everyone is known by name. One of the greatest compliments an adult can offer a three year old in the corridor at church is to call that child correctly by name. A high priority for the wise pastor who arrived only a few weeks ago is to spend at least a fourth of the time during the children's sermon addressing every child correctly by name with questions and comments. When that new pastor soon is able to identify every child correctly by name, that proves the new minister (a) is willing to make the effort to earn a sense of acceptance, (b) knows what is important, and (c) understands that title and office no longer carry the weight they once did. When a mother and father and their children come by to shake the pastor's hand after worship, the parents (a) may not even notice when that minister fails to address them by name and (b) are delighted the pastor is willing to bend down for eye-level contact with their children, calling them correctly by name.

In the big congregation, members meet one another in the corridor, and the greetings often consist of "Hi" or a nod or a smile or "Good morning" or "How're you doing?" In the healthy small church, it is more likely to be, "Hey, Dan, we missed you last Sunday. Where were you?" "Good morning, Martha, how's Jim doing? When will he be coming home from the hospital?" "You're looking great today, Terry! Married life must be agreeing with you." Many times, of course, the big difference between Sunday morning greetings in the large congregation and the small church is not only anonymity versus calling someone by name, but it also is the difference between three words and four paragraphs.

The third insight from that "Cheers" theme song is "our troubles are all the same." The church-growth specialists call that the homogeneous unit principle. The members of the small church share many things in common. By contrast, the large and numerically growing congregation often is a heterogeneous collection of homogeneous groups, classes, cells, choirs, and circles. In the small church, people expect to find homogeneity within the membership. In the healthy, large, and heterogeneous congregation, the point of homogeneity is in the group life.

The Third Place

Perhaps the best perspective for understanding the distinctive identity of the healthy small church is found in an exceptionally wise book, *The Great Good Place,* by Ray Oldenburg.[1] The author laments the disappearance of "the third place" from American culture. What is the third place? For generations most Americans lived at home (the first place in their world), journeyed to work (the second place, although for some workaholics this became their first place), and found a third place where they could relax and be identified for who they are as individuals. In the first place, we are identified by kinship roles, in the second by our job, skill, position, or title. In that wonderful third place, our identity is in who we are as a person. That tavern in "Cheers" is an excellent example of a third place.

A few generations ago millions of women living on the farm saw the women's organization in their church as their third place. For others, it was an hour or two every Saturday in the general store, where they chatted with other farm women. The farmer may have found his third place in the hardware store or the blacksmith shop. In scores of mill towns, the home was where the father had an identity by who he was as parent, husband, breadwinner, disciplinarian, and general handyman. In the mill or factory, his identity was in his job specialty or what he did. On the way home from work, he stopped in the tavern to "hoist a few with the boys." In that third place, his identity was in who he was as a human being, not in his role as a husband-father-breadwinner, nor in his role as a mechanic or spinner or welder or carpenter.

In today's world, many teenagers identify home as the first place in their lives, school as the second (work) place, and their part-time job in a fast food restaurant or the enclosed shopping mall or the gang or their car as their third place.

The best of today's churches, regardless of size, affirm the value of the third place in people's lives. For one soprano, the choir is her third place. For another member, it is an adult Sunday school class. For at least a few, the third place in their lives is the small Bible study-prayer-mutual support group they joined seven years ago that continues to meet every Tuesday evening. For several teenagers, the church youth group is their third place. For a few women, a circle in the women's organization has become their third place.

One model of the healthy small church is when one-half to two-thirds of today's members identify this as the number-one third place in their lives. Examples include the congregation composed largely of first-generation immigrants from Korea; the fundamentalist small church in Appalachia; the open country church in the Great Plains, where Sunday morning brings the same fifteen people week after week—and twelve of them were born before 1930; the closely knit congregation that meets in a large city and is organized around worship, a food pantry, intercessory prayer, a clothes closet, Bible study, advocacy ministries, mutual support groups, community outreach, fellowship, and the personality of a deeply committed and long-tenured pastor; the Presbyterian congregation in Minnesota that is the only "non-Lutheran Protestant church in this town" of 600 residents; the central city congregation in which one-half of today's adult members were born in the same county in West Virginia or Mississippi; the small church that includes a nursery-through-grade-five Christian day school with an enrollment of forty children, and the point of commonality among the members is powerful upwardly mobile ambitions for their children; or that small church that continues to raise an astonishingly large amount of money for missions annually through those big dinners—and the kitchen is the third place for six or seven women and two or three men.

What Are the Common Threads?

These three types of small churches display several common characteristics. One is that the healthy small church is not simply a small version of the large church.

This distinction was overlooked by countless new missions that were planted as small congregations with the hope that eventually they would become very large churches. "We plant the acorn today, and eventually we'll have a big oak tree," was one analogy widely used in the first half of the twentieth century. While that sequence did happen occasionally, and those highly visible examples became the basis for the hope that the model would work, a far more common pattern during the past fourteen decades has been that those new missions that did not reach an average worship attendance of two hundred by the end of year seven of their existence usually became permanent small churches. The rare exceptions usually were the result of an exceptionally gifted and dynamic pastor who brought a vision of what could be and the transformational leadership skills required to turn that vision into reality. One result is that today those who seek to create new big churches usually plan to begin with a worship attendance of at least three hundred on that first Sunday. They have learned that the best way to create large churches is to begin with a large crowd rather than with a handful of people who hope to grow. (One of the explanations for the large number of small churches today is that many new missions are still planted on the assumption that the best beginning point is to gather two or three or four dozen adults as the nucleus. This tends to attract newcomers who prefer that small intimate fellowship. This model also tends to encourage the pastor to concentrate on one-to-one relationships. When combined, those two behavioral patterns usually are effective in keeping that new mission to under one hundred in worship attendance. When the founding pastor departs, the preference of the members often is for a successor who is comfortable in a "Cheers" model or a third place or a second commandment church.)

A second common characteristic of small churches is that many of the statements about and admonitions directed to churches in general do not apply to small churches. "Every congregation should be a growing church" is one example. That may be good advice for churches averaging more than 160 at worship, but it is irrelevant to the life and ministry of the congregation that has been averaging between 25 and 40 at worship for forty years. Triple or quadruple the size of the crowd in that tavern in "Cheers," and that would destroy the reason why people come there. When 20 people gather for the noon meal in someone's home, it is no longer the first place in the lives of those present. The two or three adults who eat at that table 365 days a year are relieved when the other 17 depart. Now, for the first time in hours, or maybe even days, they can relax and be themselves.

A third common thread, and the central theme of this chapter, is that all healthy small churches seek to live out the second of what Jesus defined as the two great commandments (Matthew 22:35-40). The best small churches are organized primarily around the principle of loving your neighbor.[2]

For many people, the terms *small* and *rural* often are linked together when the discussion moves to the small church. This overlooks one of the most distinctive and one of the most valuable models. This is the small congregation that averages between forty and eighty-five adults at worship and is located in an older neighborhood in a large central city or an old suburb. The best of this model represent a combination of Robert Frost's definition of home, the "Cheers" model, a great healthy third place, and the biblical injunction to love one's neighbor. Typically, one-half to two-thirds of the adults are either never married or formerly married individuals in the 23 to 45 age bracket. Newcomers are warmly welcomed regardless of age, gender, marital status, race, sexual orientation, education, income, or theological stance. Many of the newcomers are hurting people who come hoping to be healed. When they are healed, many move on to a new environment where no one knows their previous condition. This helps to explain why observers often describe these small churches as redemptive communities or as healing centers.

The pastor, who may be part-time or full-time at a low salary partially offset by an employed spouse, often combines the roles of pastor, therapist, parental role, eccentric but beloved uncle, worship leader, facilitator, cheerleader, friend, teacher, confidant, enabler, and urban missioner. The congregation is largely a passing parade of people moving from one stage of their personal pilgrimage to a new stage in their lives. A dozen or so stable, solid, dependable, and deeply committed members provide much of the continuity and stability. These often are among the best examples of the second-commandment church.

By contrast, the best of the larger churches are organized *primarily* around the first great commandment. They are organized to respond in a meaningful manner to the religious needs of people. A secondary consideration is to create and nurture the feeling that this is a Christian community. The larger the congregation, the more likely the second great commandment will be implemented through (a) the many face-to-face groups, adult Sunday school classes; (b) an intentional, systematic and redundant system for the assimilation of new members;[3] (c) a well-organized system for world missions; (d) local community outreach ministries; (e) mission trips; (f) off-campus ministries; and (g) the ministry of music.[4]

Most newcomers, however, return week after week because of that emphasis on the first of these two great commandments. This is expressed through high-quality worship, preaching, intercessory prayer, the teaching ministries, music, modeling, missions, learning, drama, visual communication, and the challenge to discipleship.

The healthy small churches, however, are what Carl Dudley has identified as "single cell" organizations.[5] Everyone is expected to be a part of the "inner fellowship circle." The goal is that an "outer circle" will not exist. Everyone feels a sense of belonging in that single inner circle. The two most effective means of gaining that sense of belonging in the inner circle are (1) helping to pioneer the creation of that new small congregation or (2) being born into a family of one of the pioneers. A distant third is marrying into a pioneer family, and fourth is earning a place in the inner circle by works.

Before the reader becomes too upset, it should be emphasized this is not an "either-or" description. The key words are *primary* and *secondary.* The *primary,* or central organizing, principle in the healthy small church is the interaction of people with one another. A *secondary* organizing principle is a healthy, relevant, and meaningful response to the religious yearnings of people.[6] Ideally every congregation will excel in both, but that is both difficult and rare.

Where Is the Continuity?

The social ties of the people in the small church often are reinforced by kinship ties, long-standing friendships, geographical proximity, nationality, race, social class, language, local traditions, intercessory prayer, adult study groups, shared experiences, common goals, caring for one another, dinners, working together on institutional survival goals such as putting a new roof on the building, marriage, coming together weekly for the common worship of God, and missions.

The importance of social interaction is illustrated by the experiences of one small church. For seven years, this congregation was served by a minister with an average level of professional skills and an average level of competence in interpersonal relationships. Worship attendance on Sunday morning averaged seventy. The successor was at best an average preacher, but excelled in one-to-one relationships with people, was a highly productive worker, completed a thousand calls on people annually, wore a perpetual smile, rarely failed not only to call everyone correctly by name but also to inquire after family members by name, displayed an exceptionally friendly and gregarious personality, and earned a grade of C- or D+ as an administrator. Worship attendance climbed to an average of nearly ninety during that six-year pastorate.

The successor was and is a superb preacher with a deeply introverted personality who clearly prefers books to people, won the preaching award and a prize for New Testament Greek in seminary, enjoyed administration as long as meetings began and closed on schedule, and left to go back to school in hopes of becoming a teacher. During those five years, average worship attendance gradually dropped to sixty-five.

This is the seventh year in the tenure of the current pastor, who dropped out of seminary for financial reasons after two years and may never graduate. This minister is described by members as a loving and caring person, a fair administrator, the best in the county at conducting funerals, an average preacher, a superb pastor who excels in hospital visits and counseling with people in time of distress. This pastor relates exceptionally well with children and likes teenagers, but does not feel comfortable with them, so two volunteer couples staff the youth program. The pastor completes 700 to 800 calls on people annually, including hospital visits, and repeatedly has expressed a desire to continue here until retirement eighteen years hence. Most of the members share that hope, but the leaders know that is unrealistic. "The longest pastorate in the history of this church was Reverend Harrison, who served here from 1937 to 1946. What makes you think this minister will stay with us for twenty-five years? I expect any day some big church will come and make an offer that can't be refused." Worship attendance will average close to one hundred this year.

While only four pastorates in twenty-five years is not the
pattern for most small churches, that is not the crucial variable.
In this, as in most other small congregations, the continuity is
not in the minister. It is in the people, in that sacred meeting place,
in local traditions and shared experiences, in the caring, kinship
and friendship ties, and in habit.

The historical record suggests that the professional competence and the personality of the pastor have no more than a 25
percent impact, plus or minus, on the life of that small worshiping community.

Five Questions

This analogy, which uses the second great commandment to
describe the central dynamic of most long-established small
churches, does not fit every congregation. One exception, of
course, is the small parish that is organized around the Eucharist,
and where the social interaction of people is a low priority. For
most other small churches, this analogy tells only part of the
story.

It is a useful analogy, however, for responding to five frequently raised questions.

First, why do so few small churches experience numerical
growth when the population in that community is increasing at
the rate of 1 or 2 percent annually? The answer is in the analogy.
The churches most likely to reach newcomers to the community
are the first-commandment congregations that concentrate on
identifying and responding to the religious agendas of people.
To compete in that arena, the small second-commandment
church would have to change and become a first-commandment
congregation. The absence of anyone who would offer such a
motion, or second it if someone were rash enough to make it,
means that this is an unlikely possibility.

Second, why are small second-commandment churches rarely able to be transformed into first-commandment congregations?

The guiding generalization is that organizations that function largely around the interaction of people usually are far more resistant to change than are the institutions organized to produce goods or services for strangers, such as wheat, tires, milk, health care, radios, dramatic performances, technical training, corporate worship, new learning experiences, or musical performances.

Another facet of this theme is that organizations in which the primary yardstick for self-evaluation is the profit and loss statement are less resistant to change than are nonprofit organizations designed to provide services to people, such as schools, units of government, churches, hospitals, and military organizations.

A third facet is that congregations that are primarily organized around nurturing interpersonal relationships and/or building a sense of community are less likely to attract strangers than are congregations in which the top priority is identifying and providing a high-quality response to the religious needs of people.

Third, what is the best way to perpetuate the small second-commandment churches? Perhaps the single most effective strategy would be to have all future clergy in that denomination trained in theological seminaries with fewer than seventy-five people in each graduating class. A graduating class of thirty to seventy seniors offers the possibility for the students to build and enjoy that network of one-to-one relationships that is at the heart of the second-commandment churches. Keeping each graduating class to under thirty seniors would be even more effective.

If the goal is to produce effective and committed pastors who are happy in an environment filled with anonymity, complexity, and specialization, socialize them for that role in a theological seminary with at least a hundred seniors in every graduating class.

Fourth, why do so many of the longtime members drop into inactivity or switch to another church when their small second-commandment church is transformed into a first-commandment church and quadruples in size in only a few years? The answer is in the question. Those members prefer a second-commandment church. If they preferred a first-commandment church, they would have gone there originally—or switched to one when old enough to make their own decisions.

Finally, when a change of pastors occurs in a large church, why do some people leave while others stay? If the new pastor is an effective leader for a first-commandment church, nearly everyone remains. The longtime members who prefer a second-commandment church already have that in their established relationships with friends and kinfolk and in the group life of that large church. The quality of the ministry addressed to people's spiritual needs is a welcome bonus. Most of the newer members stay because they came to have their religious agenda addressed and the new minister does that in a meaningful and effective manner.

If, however, the new minister is a mismatch who really belongs in a smaller second-commandment church, many of those who perceived this to be a first-commandment church do depart. The first-time visitors who assume that because of the size this should be a first-commandment church usually do not return.

An overlapping response to this last question is that first-commandment churches often are fragile institutions, while second-commandment congregations are more resilient, tougher, and less vulnerable to disruptive actions by a new pastor.

What Are the Implications?

In today's religious culture, this means that the large and numerically growing congregations usually are (a) organized

primarily around the first of those two great commandments of
Jesus, (b) more open to change, and (c) more likely to look for
continuity in the senior minister, the program staff, and a religious agenda.

By contrast, small congregations usually are (a) organized
primarily around the second of those two great commandments, (b) more likely to resist change and innovation, and (c)
more likely to look for continuity in the members, local
traditions, denominational identity, shared experiences, kinship and friendship ties, that sacred meeting place, and a social
agenda.

This difference is expressed in congregations that are organized around the first great commandment because they are more
likely to attract and assimilate strangers than those organized
around the second great commandment.

A second difference is that the leaders in the large churches
are more likely to evaluate paid staff around professional characteristics, while the leaders in the small churches are more
likely to focus on personal characteristics than on professional
skills as leaders, innovators, preachers, sacramentalists, or administrators.

One interesting example of this is described in a study of
twenty Roman Catholic parishes that (a) do not have a resident
priest and (b) are served by resident female lay ministers. These
women are valued by their parishioners because of (a) their
ability to call each parishioner correctly by name, (b) their home
visits, (c) a collaborative leadership style, (d) a spirit of solidar-
ity, (e) their attention to the sick and dying, (f) their "pastoral
heart," (g) the shift from a hierarchical to a circular relationship
between parishioners and pastor, and (h) an affirmation of egali-
tarianism.[7] One interpretation could be that these represent
changes in the Roman Catholic Church. Another interpretation
is that these are predictable patterns when a person-centered and
extroverted minister, regardless of gender or credentials, comes

to serve the small second-commandment parish that feels it has been abandoned by the denominational leaders.

Perhaps the most significant implication of this conceptual framework can be seen in the definition of *quality*. The members of the small second-commandment church naturally tend to refer to the relational dimensions of congregational life when they boast about the quality of their church. "We're the friendliest church in town." The pastor returns from vacation and brags, "While we were gone, we worshiped with three different congregations, but none of them can match this one in the quality of the fellowship and the caring."

By contrast, the senior pastor of the large seven-day-a-week, first-commandment church returns from vacation and reports, "While we were gone, we worshiped with three different congregations in three cities. At the first one, we experienced a new model for Sunday morning worship that we should consider adding to our schedule. At the second, we met with a version of an adult Sunday school class that we could adapt to our teaching ministry. At the third, we were introduced to some new music that we could use to enrich worship here."

When the leaders of the first-commandment church discuss quality, their reference points usually include the preaching, the ministry of music, the total worship experience, the teaching ministries, the missional outreach locally, the meeting place, or the number of newcomers in the congregation.

Finally, for many small ex-neighborhood churches in urban communities, their lack of a neighborhood orientation is the result of the decisions by dozens of member households to upgrade their housing, but they continue to "drive back in to church."

By contrast, the ex-neighborhood church that is now a first-commandment regional congregation usually evolved into that role, not because a dozen or more members changed their place of residence, but rather out of a desire to reach more people with the Good News that Jesus Christ is Lord and Savior.

At this point the reader may ask, "If the first commandment was the first to be articulated by Jesus, why do we have so many small second-commandment churches?" That question requires a new chapter.

2.

WHY ARE SMALL CHURCHES SMALL?

Why are obese people fat?
While individual circumstances vary, for most adults that condition can be explained in two sentences. First, fat people take in more calories than they burn. Second, correcting that caloric imbalance requires change, and most of us obese adults are reluctant to make those changes.

Why are small churches small? First, they do those things that are appropriate for their size. Second, they are unable or unwilling to make the changes required to grow in numbers.

A parallel statement can be made. A disproportionately large number of adults on the North American continent are obese. Likewise, the vast majority of Protestant congregations on the North American continent are small. Does that mean that North Americans are destined to be overweight? No. Does that mean that most North American congregations are destined to gather fewer than a hundred people when they come together to worship God? No, those North Americans who follow a particular lifestyle will be overweight. Likewise, most of those Protestant congregations that follow a particular style of congregational life will be small. Exceptions can be found in each category, but they are few.

But What About the Demographics?

"Hold it!" exclaims one reader. "Our church is located in a rural county in the Great Plains with only a couple of thousand residents in the whole county. Every year more people move out than move in, and deaths nearly equal births. The town we're located in has only 400 residents and three churches. How do you expect us to grow?"

One answer is that those counties are an exception. Relatively few Protestant churches are located in the less populous counties.[1] A second answer is to ask what year it is. If the year is 1930, when the roads were poor and there were only 186 automobiles per 1,000 residents, it is difficult to attract people who live more than four miles away to come to your church. That is a long journey each way. If, however, the year is 1995 or 1996 or 1997, we enjoy excellent roads year around, and there are 585 passenger cars per 1,000 residents (plus an estimated 80 minivans and family-owned noncommercial pickup trucks and sports vehicles per 1,000 residents). Thus today it is not unusual for people to travel a half hour or longer each way to work, to shop, to a ball game, or to church. One consequence is that the potential service area of that small church now includes fifteen times as many people as it did in 1930. To draw people from a ten- to twenty-mile radius, however, usually requires several changes in the traditions of most small rural churches. That may be difficult to accomplish, and it may be unwise to attempt.

That is the point. For most small churches, either rural or urban, numerical growth will not happen without substantial changes. For at least a few, it means relocation of the meeting place to a more accessible and visible site. For many more, it means changing the self-image and the style of congregational life. Before examining the nature of those changes, however, it may be useful to look at several other factors.

What Is Normative?

The first factor is the most subjective. What is the normative size of congregations in American Protestantism? What is the natural or normative size of churches in this North American religious culture? One parallel is that while a growing number of women on this continent are at least six feet in height, the vast majority range between 5-feet-2-inches and 5-feet-10-inches tall. While exceptions do exist, more than three-quarters of all females, ages 25-64, on the North American continent are between 5-feet-2-inches and 5-feet-10-inches in height. (By contrast, only 55 percent of women ages 65-74 are in that height bracket, and the proportion of women who are taller than 5-feet-7-inches in height has quintupled during the past fifty years.)

For those who want to narrow it down, approximately one-half of all adult women on the North American continent are less than 5-feet-6-inches tall, and one half are taller.

Give or take three or four inches, the normative height for women on this continent is five and one-half feet.

Likewise, about half of all Protestant congregations on this continent average fewer than 75 at worship, and about half average more than 75.

Thus it could be said that the normative size of Protestant congregations on this continent is, give or take a dozen, approximately 75 people at worship on the average Sunday morning.

Means, Medians, and Modes

The range in the size of congregations among various religious traditions, however, is far greater than is the range in height among women. One way to explore that is to look at three kinds of averages. Perhaps the most useful is the median. That means one-half of the numbers in a statistical array are larger than that figure and one-half are smaller. Thus in an array of numbers from 1 through 11, 6 is the median.

The next question is over what should be measured. Since there are huge differences in how congregations define who is a member, a more uniform yardstick is worship attendance. While standards in counting do vary, that is a reasonably consistent criterion. In the Wisconsin Evangelical Lutheran Synod, for example, one-half of the parishes report an average worship attendance of 94 or less, and one-half report average worship attendance of more than 94. In the Southern Baptist Convention, that median is an average worship attendance of 75. In the Episcopal Church, the median is an average worship attendance of approximately 100, but that average is based on four reporting Sundays. United Methodists report that one-half of their congregations average more than 57 at worship and one-half average 57 or less. For the Evangelical Covenant Church, the median is approximately 135. The median is close to 110 for the Evangelical Lutheran Church in America, while it is approximately 58 for the Free Methodist Church and 120 for the Reformed Church in America.

Less useful in discussing the size of Protestant churches is the mean. This is determined by dividing the combined attendance for all congregations by the total number of reporting churches. In 1965, for example, The Methodist Church reported a combined average worship attendance of 3,886,270.

(In the same year the former Evangelical United Brethren Church reported a combined average worship attendance of 421,000 in 4,200 congregations for a mean average of 100.) When that Methodist total is divided by the 38,500 reporting congregations, the mean average was approximately 101.

A quarter of a century later, in 1990, a total of 36,540 congregations (out of a total of 37,295 organized churches) in the newly merged denomination reported a combined worship attendance of 3,466,439 for a mean average of 95. That represented a 5 percent shrinkage in the mean in a quarter of a century.

The 34,975 Southern Baptist congregations reporting their worship attendance in 1990 reported a combined total attendance of 4,575,789 for a mean average of 131. An equally useful Southern Baptist figure is that the one thousand largest congregations reported a combined total worship attendance of nearly one million, the same combined total attendance as experienced by the 20,000 smallest congregations.

In 1990, 11,000 congregations in the Evangelical Lutheran Church in America reported a combined average worship attendance of 1,636,860 for a mean average of 149. That compared with a mean average of 352 confirmed members per congregation for a worship attendance-to-membership ratio of 42 percent.

The least useful of these three averages is the mode. This is the number that occurs most frequently in a series. In a survey of 21 Protestant denominations in the United States, five denominations reported that 50 was the average worship attendance reported most frequently, in two the mode was 45, in three it was 40, in three others it was 35, and in three it was 30. The largest mode was 75 in the Evangelical Free Church, and the smallest was 25 in The United Methodist Church, where 964 reported 25 as their average worship attendance in 1990, compared to 948 that reported 40, 739 that reported 50 as their average, and only 552 that reported an average worship attendance of 500 or more.

These three sets of averages all support the broad generalization that the normative size for Protestant congregations in this culture is an average worship attendance of 75, more or less.

Where Are the Small Churches?

That generalization must be tempered, however, by recognizing the differences among various religious traditions in American Protestantism. This can be illustrated by looking at twenty-one Protestant denominations. In broad general terms, the typical Protestant denomination reports that approximately one-tenth of all of its congregations will include 25 or fewer worshipers on the typical Sunday. The accompanying table reports the differences among these denominations. The United Methodist Church, which in recent years has been increasing both the number and the proportion of small churches, leads the list with more than one-fifth of its congregations in the very small church category. At the other extreme, five other denominations report these very small churches account for only 4 percent of all of their congregations. (CAUTION: In several denominations a significant number of congregations do not report their worship attendance. These nonreporting churches come in disproportionately large numbers from among smaller congregations. Therefore, for several denominations this table underreports the proportion of small churches. It also should be noted that the reporting systems are not identical. For Southern Baptist congregations, the figure is the worship attendance in the Sunday closest to the reporting date. For Episcopal parishes, it is the average of four Sundays.)

PROPORTION OF
CONGREGATIONS REPORTING
WORSHIP ATTENDANCE OF
25 OR LESS IN 1991

United Methodist Church	21%
Free Methodist Church	19
Church of God (Anderson, Indiana)	14
Church of the Nazarene	13
Presbyterian Church (U.S.A.)	13
Assemblies of God	12
Church of the Brethren	12
American Baptist Churches	11
Southern Baptist Convention	11
Christian (Disciples of Christ)	10
Episcopal Church	10
Presbyterian Church in America	9
North American Baptist Conference	9
United Church of Christ	9
Wisconsin Evangelical Lutheran Synod	5
Evangelical Lutheran Church in America	5
Lutheran Church-Missouri Synod	4
Evangelical Free Church	4
Baptist General Conference	4
Reformed Church in America	4
Evangelical Covenant Church	4

What Are the Proportions?

Perhaps the best perspective for looking at this question of normative size is to compare extremes. Thus for every three women, ages 35-44, in the United States who are under five feet in height, there also are three who are at least five-feet-ten-inches tall.

SMALL AND LARGE CHURCHES

Denomination	Ratio
American Baptist Church	36 to 1
Assemblies of God	20 to 1
Baptist General Conference	10 to 1
Christian Church (Disciples of Christ)	116 to 1
Church of God, Anderson	141 to 1
Church of the Brethren	126 to 1
Church of the Nazarene	35 to 1
Episcopal Church	13 to 1
Evangelical Covenant Church	12 to 1
Evangelical Free Church	9 to 1
Evangelical Lutheran Church in America	19 to 1
Free Methodist	62 to 1
Lutheran Church-Missouri Synod	9 to 1
N. American Baptist Conference	22 to 1
Presbyterian Church in America	12 to 1
Presbyterian Church (U.S.A.)	24 to 1
Reformed Church in America	8 to 1
Southern Baptist Convention	20 to 1
United Church of Christ	87 to 1
United Methodist	47 to 1
Wisconsin Evangelical Lutheran Synod	8 to 1

Note: In several denominations many of the smaller congregations did not report worship attendance.

That distribution is radically different for churches! For example, if an average worship attendance of 100 or fewer is used to define "small" and over 500 is used to define "large," what is the ratio of small to large?

For every Church of the Brethren congregation averaging over 500 at worship, there are 126 that average fewer than a hundred. At the other end of that scale are the Reformed Church in America and the Wisconsin Evangelical Lutheran Synod, in which there are only eight small congregations for every large one. The accompanying table reports this ratio for twenty-one other denominations.

What Is the 67th Percentile!

Finally, it may be useful to take one more look at the distribution of congregations by size. What proportion of the churches in American Protestantism average more than a hundred at worship? One answer is that it depends. A few religious traditions are large church denominations. The Evangelical Free Church and the Reformed Church in America are examples. Others are small church traditions. The Free Methodist Church, The United Methodist Church, and the Church of the Brethren are examples of small-church religious traditions.

A second answer to that question is that about 40 percent of all Protestant churches on this continent average more than a hundred at worship. (That may be high since we do not have comprehensive data on storefront congregations and house churches. It is possible that no more than 30 percent of the estimated 325,000 Protestant congregations in the United States average more than a hundred at worship. The small independent congregations are far less likely to be counted in a census of religious bodies than are small denominationally related churches.)

A third answer is to choose the 67th percentile as the dividing line. The largest one-third are at or above that line, and the smallest two-thirds are below it. What is that line? It varies tremendously, and for some traditions it is more than double the 67th percentile in others. For five large and predominantly Anglo Protestant bodies in North America (the Southern Baptist Convention [38,000 congregations], The United Methodist Church [37,000 congregations], the Assemblies of God [11,600 congregations], the Presbyterian Church [U.S.A.] [11,400 congregations], and the Evangelical Lutheran Church in America [11,000 congregations]), the range of the 67th percentile is between 87 and 157. These five denominations include 109,000 congregations, or one-third of all of the churches in American Protestantism. The 67th percentile for those 109,000 congregations is approximately 110 at worship on the typical Sunday.

THE 67th PERCENTILE

Two-thirds of the congregations in the following denominations average less than the number given at worship, and one-third average this number or more.

Evangelical Free Church	201
Reformed Church in America	176
Episcopal Church	165
Lutheran Church-Missouri Synod	160
Evangelical Lutheran Church in America	157
Baptist General Conference	155
Wisconsin Evangelical Lutheran Church	142
Evangelical Covenant Church	140
Presbyterian Church in America	127
Presbyterian Church (U.S.A.)	124
United Church of Christ	120
American Baptist Churches	116
Southern Baptist Convention	110
Disciples of Christ	110
Church of the Nazarene	105
Assemblies of God	100
Church of God, Anderson	99
North American Baptist Conference	98
Church of the Brethren	93
United Methodist Church	87
Free Methodist Church	73

Why Is It That Way?

At this point, the impatient reader may interrupt, "You have persuaded me that the normative size for Protestant congregations in the United States is fewer than a hundred people at worship, but you have failed to explain why it is that way. Why isn't the normative size two hundred or three hundred at worship?"

Perhaps the best answer to that question is this: "It's always been that way." For more than three centuries, following the arrival of the first Christians from Europe, Protestant congregations have been substantially smaller than Roman Catholic parishes. These comparatively small Protestant congregations fit comfortably into a society that for centuries was dominated by small institutions. The small Protestant congregation fit the same scale as the small farm, the small retail store, and the small public elementary school.

A second, and perhaps more influential, part of the explanation is that nearly all of the 325,000 Protestant congregations in the United States began their institutional life as small churches. They began as small churches and never changed. Only during the past three decades has anyone dreamed the dream of planting new missions that were large congregations from day one.

Perhaps the most influential single factor has been the model. The three most widely followed models in American Protestantism have been (1) a congregation with only one paid staff person, the full-time resident pastor; (2) the congregation served by one part-time paid pastor who either served one or more other churches or had secular employment; and (3) the congregation with no paid staff, served by volunteer leaders. All three are small-church models.

A fourth part of the explanation is that most theological seminaries have trained future parish pastors on the assumption that their first assignment following graduation will be to serve one or more small congregations. That reinforced the self-fulfilling prophecy. The faculty in most seminaries also modeled the individual leader model and/or the lone superstar model rather than a leadership team style that is appropriate for many larger congregations.

The fifth factor is the sum of the first four variables and is also the central theme of this book. For the small, second-commandment congregation to grow into a big church usually requires a transformation into a first-commandment church. That is not an easy change! It is especially difficult when the institutional reward system applauds the ordained minister who excels as a pastor, rather than as the initiator of planned change.

The sixth, and perhaps most subtle, factor was that up until about 1960 the focus in most Protestant traditions was either on (a) taking care of the members or (b) converting nonbelievers. It was not on initiating the changes required to accommodate more people or to assimilate newcomers or to transform the second-commandment congregation into a first-commandment church.

Converting the nonbeliever is an ancient strand in the fabric of American Protestantism. Deliberately transforming a long-established small congregation into a big church is a recent patch that was devised to cover a hole that most believed did not exist in the cloth covering their denomination.

A seventh factor, which rarely is discussed openly, is the reluctance of church leaders to accept the fact that the privately owned automobile is here to stay. Leaders who daily spend fifteen to forty minutes in the journey to work often are reluctant to affirm that people can be expected to drive ten to twenty minutes to church.

In a few traditions, an eighth variable has been the recent surplus of clergy. A dozen congregations, each averaging 75 to 100 at worship, will provide more jobs for ordained ministers than will be offered by one church averaging 800 to 1,000 at worship. The small churches are needed to provide adult employment opportunities for the clergy.

Finally, in several religious traditions a widespread antilarge-church prejudice has encouraged the creation and perpetuation of smaller congregations. One expression of this attitude is to focus on representing institutions and the clergy, rather than lay members, at annual denominational meetings. Another has been to expect the large congregations to provide the money required to subsidize small churches. Economists have long advised that what is taxed will decrease in numbers while that which is subsidized will increase.

While far from an exhaustive list, these are a few of the factors that help to explain why the normative size of a Protestant congregation in the United States is around seventy-five people at worship, rather than two or three or four hundred.

Are Small Churches an Endangered Species?

One issue in any discussion of the future of small churches is the definition of that word *small*. For this book, the definition is "fewer than a hundred at worship." That definition includes close to 60 percent of all Protestant congregations on the North American continent.

A second question raised by many concerns the relevance of the discussion. Dozens of church-growth specialists and other observers of the ecclesiastical landscape contend that small churches are on the road to extinction. They cannot survive in an increasingly competitive ecclesiastical environment. The small church belongs on the same list with the California gnat-catcher, the northern spotted owl, the pug nose shiner, and other endangered species. That generalization greatly oversimplifies a complex issue.

The small church is not an endangered species! While it is true that the average (mean) size of Protestant congregations at the end of the twentieth century is at least three times the average (mean) size in 1900, that tells only part of the story. The number of small Protestant churches averaging fewer than a hundred at worship continues to increase, but at a slower pace than the increase in the number of Protestant churchgoers. There are more very large congregations than ever before in American history, and they are attracting a growing proportion of the churchgoers born after 1955. Small congregations, however, continue to account for approximately one-third of all Protestant churchgoers on the typical weekend.

In a few traditions, the total number of congregations has been shrinking, while the number of small churches has been increasing. The most highly visible example of this trend is The United Methodist Church. In 1974 this denomination reported 39,195 congregations, down from 40,653 in 1970. The number of congregations reporting an average worship attendance of 34 or fewer, however, increased by over a thousand, from 9,741 in 1974 to 10,897 in 1990, despite a drop of nearly two thousand in the number of congregations to 37,295 at the end of 1990. A drop of nearly 5 percent in the number of congregations was accompanied by an increase of 11 percent in the number of very small congregations.

The small church is the heart of several smaller Protestant religious traditions, such as the Reorganized Church of Jesus Christ of Latter Day Saints. Most of their thousand congregations average fewer than seventy-five at worship. The Reformed Episcopal Church averages fewer than one hundred members per parish. Two-fifths of the 787 congregations in the Cumberland Presbyterian Church report fifty or fewer active members. Scores of other small denominations are composed largely of small congregations.

The truly endangered species among the small Protestant churches in the United States include seven categories. One is the new mission that plateaus at an average worship attendance of forty or less and never reaches its seventh birthday. A second is the small immigrant parish that cannot attract the children and grandchildren of the charter members.

A third is the congregation that averages 60 to 120 at worship and no longer can afford a full-time resident pastor. The compensation for the clergy has been rising at a faster pace than the increase in the members' income. These congregations are being priced out of the ministerial marketplace. One alternative is to grow in numbers and thus strengthen the financial base. That is not the most attractive appeal, however, for bringing in new members! A second alternative is to change the style of congregational life in order to attract more people, but those changes seldom receive the required support. A third is to merge with another congregation. A fourth option is to abandon the dream of being served by a full-time resident pastor. A fifth is to close.

A fourth endangered species overlaps the second and third categories. This group consists of those congregations that no longer have a viable reason to exist. One example is what once was a first-generation immigrant congregation. A second is the Anglo congregation founded to serve an all-white constituency who lived in that center-city neighborhood. The combination of (a) the automobile, (b) the exodus of the white residents to the suburbs, (c) the influx of black or Latino or Asian residents, and (d) the inability of that congregation's leadership to define a new role means that many of these small congregations drift onto the list of endangered species.

One version of this road to extinction is the reasonably healthy second-commandment congregation that calls a new pastor to help transform it into a first-commandment church. During this painful process, the congregation is polarized, and that new pastor becomes the victim and is sacrificed. The successor is unable to resolve the conflict and departs. The next minister is a severe mismatch; many members who dislike perpetual internal conflict leave, and the institutional strength dissipates. What once was a healthy, second-commandment congregation has become a caricature of a first-commandment church. It repels those who seek either model. The resulting loss of identity erodes the loyalty of the old timers and repels potential newcomers. Ecclesiastical euthanasia becomes the most attractive option.

A fifth variation on this theme is the product of a denominational merger. One congregation, representing one of those two merged religious traditions, was the only church of that denomination in the community. Across the street is the meeting place of a congregation affiliated with the other tradition. Following the merger, they share a common denominational identity. One alternative is for each to carve out a distinctive ministry that distinguishes it from the sister church across the street. An easier option is to drift in a goalless fashion from crisis to crisis until the list of choices has been reduced to two: Should we merge with our neighbor or disband? We are too weak to relocate. We are too attached to yesterday to carve out a new role to reach new generations. What can we do?

A sixth category overlaps the fourth and fifth and is by far the most varied. These are the small churches that seek to do yesterday over again and find they cannot match the competition from other churches in a rapidly changing and often hostile urban environment. Most of the people who appreciate their approach to ministry are now in retirement villages, nursing homes, and cemeteries. The attachment of these small churches to the past, coupled with that hostile urban setting, places them on the endangered species list.

The last of these seven categories is the small congregation affiliated with a denomination that is organized around a "connectional" polity, such as Roman Catholic or Presbyterian or United Methodist. In these traditions, the denomination possesses the authority to close churches. The best study of this was conducted three decades ago in 99 rural townships in Missouri. The number of Presbyterian and Methodist congregations in these 99 rural townships decreased between 1952 and 1982, while the number with a congregational polity increased. It also should be noted that the number of congregations affiliated with a "mainline" Protestant denomination dropped by 13.8 percent during these three decades, while the number of "non-mainline," including independent churches, increased by 15.6 percent.[2]

The small church is not an endangered species as long as it can respond to the religious and personal agendas of new generations. It is, however, an endangered species if and when the top priority becomes (a) providing full-time employment with a competitive compensation package for a full-time and fully credentialed resident pastor and/or (b) implementing denominationally formulated goals.

The small church also may be placed on the endangered species list when one or more of these conditions prevail: (a) The recently arrived pastor becomes convinced that dissolution or merger is the most viable course of action; (b) it is affiliated with a denomination in which the leadership possesses the authority to close churches; (c) the congregation is unable or unwilling to make the changes required to reach and serve new generations of potential constituents; (d) the leaders conclude dissolution or merger is preferable to change; and/or (e) the small congregation becomes increasingly dependent on an annual financial subsidy from the denominational headquarters—the sudden removal of that financial subsidy can be equivalent to ecclesiastical euthanasia.

From a denominational perspective, two other threats to the small church also should be mentioned. The most unlikely is that every denomination will cease to plant new small missions, and each one will concentrate only on planting new congregations that include at least three hundred worshipers from day one. That not only is unlikely to happen, but that scenario also requires every new mission to be a success story.

A more likely scenario already is beginning to unfold. Once upon a time pastors, teachers, and nurses identified themselves as called to a vocation that required considerable personal sacrifice. In recent years, however, an increasing number of nurses and teachers identify themselves as professionals who should be compensated at the same level as other professionals. In those religious traditions in which new generations of clergy identify themselves as professionals who should be compensated as professionals, it will be increasingly difficult to provide seminary trained and fully credentialed clergy to serve as resident pastors. As that trend continues, the result may be to endanger the future of thousands of small churches. A more likely result, however, is that it will endanger the career dreams of more pastors than congregations as these small churches choose a bivocational pastor or bivocational ministerial team.

During the first half of the twentieth century, the biggest threat to small churches was concealed in two of the most enticing words in the ecclesiastical dictionary: *cooperation* and *efficiency*. But that discussion requires another chapter that also lifts up the differences between second-commandment congregations and first-commandment churches.

3.

COMPETE OR COOPERATE?

When I became the senior pastor here back in 1958, I recognized that we would be competing with the six other churches of our denomination for new members," recalled a seventy-four-year-old minister who had returned with his wife to the large downtown congregation they once had served for twenty-two years. After two subsequent pastorates, they decided to "come back home" to enjoy the role of "minister emeritus" in their retirement years.

"For the most part, those six other churches had an advantage over us in their geographical proximity to where newcomers to the city lived, and three of them also had a surplus of off-street parking," explained this veteran minister, "but we had a stronger program. Nearly everyone agreed we had the best chancel choir in the city, one of the three best pipe organs in the whole state, a full Sunday school with eight or nine adult classes, and, if I do say so myself, excellent preaching. Despite our lack of off-street parking, we were competitive. Bethany was the only church of our denomination in the city that could match us in the number of new members received annually. About half the time in the years we were here, Bethany led the seven churches of our denomination in this city in the number of new members received, and about half the years we led."

"How does that compare with today?" asked the associate minister, who had arrived three weeks earlier.

"Two big differences," came the immediate response. "First, this congregation helped start a new church on the west side of the city in 1961 and one on the north side in 1969. They now rank first and fourth in membership among the churches of our denomination here. About ten years ago, the west side church passed us in membership. Those two, plus Bethany, are the only churches from this denomination that really compete with us for new members today.

"Second, and more important, our biggest competition comes not from churches of our own denomination, but from the four megachurches here. First Presbyterian, University Church, Calvary Temple, and Church of the Servant each averages well over fifteen hundred at worship every weekend. Those four represent our real competition today."

"How do you know that?" inquired this new associate minister.

"For years this church has had an excellent system for securing the names and addresses of all first-time visitors," replied this retired pastor. "When we moved back here, I asked the senior minister what I could do to be helpful. After we talked about several possibilities, I suggested that I would be interested in following up on the first-time visitors who do not return. My wife and I enlisted five other volunteers. Every Tuesday we meet and go over the list of first-time visitors from fifteen weeks earlier. If they have returned at least once, they are still the responsibility of our evangelism committee. We take those that have not returned at least once and who also have a local address. That usually runs between two and twelve households per week. We divide the names among us, and each one is called. We ask for an appointment to call on them. If we can't get that, we interview them over the telephone. A few refuse to even talk with us, but most are cordial. We found that about half of those first-time visitors have ended up in one of those four megachurches, about a third are in some other church, and about a sixth are still church shopping. We encourage the senior minister or our minister of evangelism to call on those who are still shopping, and some of them eventually do join here."

"That's a lot of work!" exclaimed the new associate minister.

"Yes, it is," agreed this energetic retiree, "but we learn a lot. About a third of those we call allow us to come interview them. Out of those interviews, we have picked up a lot of suggestions on how to improve what we do here. I could write a book on what we have learned from those interviews."

Four Lessons

Four lessons stand out in this account that should be of interest to anyone concerned about the contemporary state of American Protestantism.

Perhaps the most obvious is that what once was intradenominational competition for new members has now become interdenominational. One of the fruits of the ecumenical movement of the past four decades is the continued erosion of denominational and congregational loyalties. According to the Princeton Religious Research Center, this has had a tremendous impact on Catholic, Methodist, and Baptist churches. In proportion to membership, they have bade farewell to the most members switching to another denomination or faith.[1]

A second lesson is the emergence of that rapidly growing number of megachurches that compete successfully with denominationally affiliated churches for new members. That is a relatively new pattern.

The third and oldest lesson is that competition for new members has been a part of urban church life for generations. The big difference is that pattern of intercongregational competition is far more common today than it was back in the 1950s. The competition is greater, and fewer churches are unaffected by it. The increase in the number of automobiles per 1,000 residents, the widespread expectation that everyone should enjoy the freedom of choice, the erosion of inherited institutional loyalties, the increased number of marriages across denominational and faith lines, and the contemporary demand for quality are five of the reasons behind this greater degree of competition among the churches for new members.

A fourth, and the most widely ignored, lesson is that much can be learned from interviews with people who visited your church once or twice but never returned.

Two Other Lessons

Two other lessons should be of special interest to leaders in smaller congregations.

The first is that most leaders in the larger congregations accept the fact that competition among the churches is a part of contemporary reality. Some of the older members wistfully regret that competition has replaced cooperation, but most younger leaders do not question that. By contrast, many leaders in smaller churches, and a significant number of denominational policy makers, appear to operate on the assumption that interchurch cooperation should be the dominant characteristic of the ecclesiastical scene, rather than competition.

It is only a minor exaggeration to suggest that this is one of the most influential differences between large and numerically growing congregations and most small churches. The former assume that competition is the norm. The latter believe that cooperation should be the norm. That difference in perspective is one more reason why large congregations are large and small churches are small!

The second of these two lessons can best be stated in terms of a policy question. Do we, as a small church, plan around a theme of competition with other churches in this community or around a theme of cooperation?

This is a real issue on the contemporary ecclesiastical scene. In several denominations, the operational policy that now prevails can be stated very simply. If a small congregation is not able to match the competition with other churches in that never-ending quest for new members to replace those who die, drop out, or move away, it should begin to explore the creation of cooperative arrangements with other congregations. In several annual conferences in The United Methodist Church, for example, this has become the official response to continued numerical decline in smaller congregations. If you cannot compete, cooperate!

A Strategy That Failed

Populism was one of the reform movements that emerged after the Civil War to combat the social, political, and economic ills of American society. Populism aroused considerable middle class hostility. As Eric Goldman pointed out, the populists were perceived as the party of failure, and middle class reformers preferred to identify with success.[2]

Out of this conflict, a new reform movement emerged under the label of "progressivism." The progressive reformers in the early twentieth century had a long agenda. One item was the product of the millions of people moving from rural communities to the cities. Many of the rural reformers of the Progressive Era concentrated their studies on what were widely perceived to be the two anchors of rural America: the public schools and the churches.

While many of these reformers had been born and reared in rural America, most had moved to an urban environment for both their education and their occupation. Therefore, they functioned as "outside" agents of planned change, not as "insiders." They brought an urban perspective and an urban value system to both the diagnosis and the prescription of rural ills. One of the basic assumptions advanced by these reformers was that the people would be better served and the churches would be stronger if competition could be minimized.[3] As one historian has pointed out, these reformers came to rural America with a liberal theological stance, an urban perspective, a passion for ecumenism, a predisposition to instruct rather than to listen, a commitment to efficiency, and the dream that rural churches would seek to emulate the best of the city churches.[4]

By 1920 these early reformers had concluded that rural churches were exceptionally inefficient social institutions, that cooperative action was the key to efficiency, and that rural America was deplorably overchurched.

By 1936, the situation appeared to be so bad that one of the foremost rural sociologists of that era, J. Edmund de S. Brunner, concluded that competition among the rural and small town churches "splits communities, prevents a better unified social life, results in small, inefficient congregations, poorly paid ministers, barren programs."

By 1940, it was clear to every rational, open-minded, efficiency-driven, future-oriented, thoughtful, reasonably well-educated, and progressive pastor and denominational policy maker that rural America was seriously overchurched and underserved.

It also was perfectly obvious that the most logical course of action would be to encourage the consolidation of these small rural churches into larger, more efficient, and more effective units.

A similar diagnosis and prescription was being made for the one-room public school. Between 1916 and 1956, the number of one-teacher public schools dropped from over 200,000 to under 35,000. The number of public school districts with taxing authority decreased from 127,422 in 1932 to 54,773 in 1956 to fewer than 15,500 in 1990. The authority of government turned school consolidation from a dream of the reformers into reality in two generations. One product of the consolidation of public schools has been the almost total elimination of the small elementary school with one or two teachers and fewer than sixty students. A second has been a sharp increase in the level of anonymity, anomie, alienation, and social disorganization or violence in literally thousands of large public schools. A third product of the consolidation of public schools has been a sharp increase in the number of Protestant parents enrolling their children in private schools. A fourth has been a phenomenal increase in the number of highly educated parents who choose the home schooling alternative for their children. A fifth product has been the huge increase in the size of the bureaucracy in public school districts.

Why did a similar consolidation of rural churches not occur? One answer is that it did. At least 50,000 small rural Methodist, Presbyterian, Northern Baptist, Congregational, Christian (Disciples of Christ), and Reformed congregations were closed, disbanded, or merged between 1910 and 1960.

Why was that number not higher? One reason was the absence of that centralized governmental authority that forced public schools to consolidate. A second was the opposition of a majority of rural pastors. A third was the opposition of the vast majority of the members of those small rural congregations. A fourth was that those progressive reformers eventually found other causes to promote.

Why did these pastors and rural church members object to the consolidation of the churches? From this vantage point in time, it is easy to list a dozen factors: (1) It was not their idea; (2) the natural distrust of outside experts who came with their own criteria for evaluation and their own agenda to promote; (3) inept and counterproductive strategies of intervention; (4) the threat to one of the few remaining cohesive and unifying social institutions in rural America; (5) to use the analogy presented in chapter 1, the perception that the goal was to transform these second-commandment congregations into first-commandment churches; (6) a failure to respect congregational autonomy; (7)

a bad diagnosis of the nature of small churches—as Carl Dudley and others have pointed out, the top priority of members of small churches is not efficiency, but the hope that "our pastor loves the Lord and also loves every one of us"; (8) a natural, normal, and predictable reluctance to support institutional change; (9) the increased dollar costs for these large consolidated churches; (10) the clash of value systems between the reformers and the local leaders; (11) the effort to impose an urban model on rural America; and (12) the failure to affirm the importance of "the third place" (see chapter 1) in the lives of individual churchgoers.

The survivor of those battles over the consolidation of rural churches may add another dozen factors to that list.

What Happened?

Nine decades of studies of small churches with this emphasis on cooperation produced many changes. One is the closing of thousands of small churches, both urban and rural. A second is an uncounted number of mergers that united two or three or four small congregations.

A third was the emergence of comity agreements among several of the large denominations during the first half of the twentieth century. These comity agreements were designed to minimize competition among new missions and between new missions and long-established churches. One unanticipated product of these comity arrangements has been to leave scores of choice sites for new missions available to noncooperative religious bodies and independent churches. That ideal site was too close to the building housing an established church affiliated with a cooperating denomination. Therefore, it was necessary to choose a second-best or third-best location for the site of this new mission by a cooperating denomination. That left the ideal site to be purchased and developed by a noncooperating denomination or an independent church.[5]

A fourth result has been a sharp increase in the proportion of rural (and urban) Protestant congregations that are not affiliated with any of the mainline denominations. As the total number of residents of rural America continued to increase (from 41 million in 1890 to 57 million in 1940), and as the mainline denominations followed the advice of the reformers to consolidate, cooperate, and reduce the number of their churches, the resulting vacuum was filled by new independent churches and congregations affiliated with the newer religious traditions, such as the Churches of Christ; the Assemblies of God; the Church of God, Cleveland, Tennessee; the Church of the Nazarene; the Salvation Army; the Free Will Baptists, and others.[6]

The Southern Baptist Convention also increased the number of its organized congregations from 19,558 in 1900 to 27,788 in 1950 to nearly 39,000 in 1994. By contrast, the United Church of Christ cut back from 8,800 congregations in the four predecessor denominations in 1906 to fewer than 6,400 in 1994. The United Methodists cut back from slightly over 56,000 congregations in the six predecessor denominations in 1906 to slightly over 37,000 in 1994. The Presbyterian Church (U.S.A.) counted approximately 14,000 congregations in the predecessor denominations in 1906, compared to 11,400 in 1994. In each example, the cutback is greater than it first appears because of the huge number of new congregations organized by each denomination between 1906 and 1994.

The net result of this century-long cooperative effort by several mainline denominations to control the number of new churches has been (a) a reduction in the proportion of all Protestant congregations affiliated with one of these cooperative denominations, (b) an aging of the membership in most of these cooperative denominations, (c) a net decline in the number of members and congregations affiliated with one of these cooperative denominations, and (d) the decision by a disproportionately large number of the people born after 1955 to affiliate with a new mission not related to one of these cooperative denominations.

A fifth result was the belated recognition that "overchurched communities" reach more people with the gospel of Jesus Christ than is the pattern where that "ideal" ratio of one congregation per 1,000 residents prevails. In the mid-1920s, J. Edmund de S. Brunner reported an average of 43 members per church in those communities with four or more congregations per 1,000 population, compared to an average of only 27 members per church where there was only one church per 1,000 residents, or 36 members per church where the ratio was two congregations per 1,000 residents. Similar studies in the middle third of the twentieth century reported the same basic pattern. The greater the number of congregations per 1,000 residents, the larger the proportion of the population who are regular churchgoers.

The parallel pattern is that when only one congregation of a particular denomination existed in a specific community, it usually was not doing as well, in terms of membership and attendance, as when there were two or three churches of that denomination in those communities. Intradenominational competition tends to be more supportive of the religious health of a congregation than is a denominational monopoly.

For smaller congregations, however, the most far-reaching consequence of the work of the progressive reformers in the first half of the twentieth century, plus the ecumenical movement of the second half, has been to elevate to holy status the goal of interchurch cooperation.[7]

A few cynics will quarrel with that paragraph as being overly simplistic. They insist that interchurch cooperation thrives when the context is enriched by (a) a shortage of financial resources and (b) a surplus of professionalism among the clergy.

One consequence of this series of events in the twentieth century is that small congregations, both urban and rural, are more likely to attach a high priority to interchurch cooperation than are large churches. The leaders in these large churches usually agree that an enhancement of the quality of ministry and/or an increase in the range of attractive choices offered to people is the most fruitful response to competition. This is in contrast to the ecclesiastical reformers who advocate interchurch cooperation as the ideal counter to the rising level of competition among the churches.

Seven Forms of Cooperation

Is interchurch cooperation good or bad? It depends on the form of cooperation and on the criteria used for subsequent evaluation. Perhaps the most productive expression of interchurch cooperation is when large numbers of congregations band together to create a united front on a specific national public policy issue. The antislavery movement of the middle of the nineteenth century, the prohibition movement at the turn of the century and the early years of the twentieth century, the civil rights movement of the 1960s, the public debate about abortion on demand of the last quarter of the twentieth century, and the cooperative efforts in the last quarter of the twentieth century to alleviate world hunger are examples of productive interchurch cooperation.

The newest, and also one of the most productive, expressions of interchurch cooperation is in the recent emergence of scores of self-identified mentoring churches. The leaders in these congregations invite both paid staff and volunteer leaders from other churches to come and learn from one another's experiences. The "mentors" learn as they are forced to reflect on and systematize in their own minds what they did and why it worked as well as from the questions asked by the learners. The visitors learn both from the host leader and from one another.

The big wave of interchurch cooperation that is most impressive can be seen all across the North American continent. Several congregations band together to combine their resources to feed the hungry, to shelter the homeless, to care for battered wives, to create a hospice for people dying from an AIDS-related illness, to offer after-school programs for children, to help the unemployed find new jobs, to teach basic literacy skills, to organize and support pastoral counseling centers, and/or to operate a halfway house.[8]

A fourth productive form of interchurch cooperation parallels that when the coalition of congregations is organized around advocacy rather than social welfare. These coalitions focus on state and local issues such as welfare reform, housing, taxation, pornography, public education, gambling, or health care.

A fifth and highly productive expression of interchurch cooperation reminds us of the early nineteenth century, when congregations came together to create cooperative foreign mission agencies. The current versions of this include (a) hundreds of independent congregations working together in world missions through one or more parachurch agencies; (b) two or three congregations affiliated with the same denomination working together to plant new missions; (c) scores of congregations coming together to create a new network to minister to the unchurched, such as the Willow Creek Association; (d) three or four congregations that share in two or three leadership training events annually that are created and staffed by these cooperating congregations; and (e) Churches United in Global Mission, a coalition of several score congregations from all points on the theological spectrum who have come together on behalf of world missions. Each one of these parallels a pattern from the early nineteenth century that led to strong denominational systems.

It is important to note that the second, third, fourth, and fifth of these expressions of intercongregational cooperation are based on an abundance of discretionary resources, including volunteer leadership, staff time, energy, vision, enthusiasm, money, and idealism in congregational coffers.

A sixth expression of interchurch cooperation that appears to be less common in the 1990s than it was in the 1970s is concerned with local congregational ministries. These four congregations operate a cooperative vacation Bible school every July. These three churches rotate annually the building in which the joint Thanksgiving service will be held every November. The pastor of one congregation goes on vacation every July, so the pastor and the people from the partner church come to that building for joint worship every Sunday in July. In August, the pattern is reversed. The church whose pastor is on vacation that month hosts the pastor and people from the other congregation every Sunday morning. These three congregations that are growing older in the age of the members and smaller in numbers decide to cooperate and create one youth group for teenagers from all three churches. These two churches rotate back and forth the annual Good Friday worship experience. These five congregations from the same denominational family run one combined advertisement on the religion page of the Saturday newspaper. These six small congregations jointly sponsor the appearance of an evangelist who preaches the revival service in Church A on Sunday evening, in Church B on Monday evening, in Church C on Tuesday evening, and finally in Church F on Friday evening. Members from all six congregations are urged to attend all six services, but some attend only the one scheduled for their own church.

What do these expressions of cooperation have in common? Each (a) represents an effort to encourage interchurch cooperation, (b) turns what could be entry points for prospective new members for one congregation into community service ventures, (c) usually results in smaller numbers of participants than parallel unilateral efforts would produce, (d) blurs the distinctive identity of each participating congregation, and (e) usually illustrates the axiom that intercongregational cooperation in programming is rarely compatible with numerical growth.

Finally, another expression of interchurch cooperation is for two or more congregations to share the financial cost of a full-time pastor or a ministerial staff, including one or more specialists. These efforts parallel the functional approach to parish ministry advocated by the progressive reformers in the first half of the twentieth century. The reformers encountered great frustration as they sought support for a highly profession-alized and functional model of ministry and were rebuffed by parishioners who preferred a relational emphasis.

The contemporary parallel is the person who is delighted that each visit to a doctor at that medical clinic results in an appoint-ment with a highly trained specialist, but rarely does the patient see the same physician twice. That approach to the delivery of health-care service contrasts with the patient who has been treated by the same family doctor for forty years and is com-pletely happy with that relationship.

Those who are comfortable thinking about the practice of ministry in functional or professional terms can build a persua-sive argument on behalf of the three-church yoked field or the larger parish with a staff team that services two dozen small congregations.

Those who are convinced that most churches are organized around the second of Jesus' two great commandments, who believe that smaller congregations place a premium on long-term, one-to-one relationships and who also see that much of the continuity in congregational life is in the pastor can build a persuasive argument for one minister, or one ministry team, serving only one congregation. This often means a long-tenured bivocational minister, or ministry team, who becomes the suc-cessor to the arrangement where one minister serves two or three congregations concurrently.

Another parallel is the person who is extremely ill with a rare disease that appears to be fatal. That patient usually will be eager to be treated by the stranger who has specialized in that disease and is able to promise survival.

By contrast, the person with a headache or a pain in the stomach may prefer to make an appointment with the family doctor who has treated this patient successfully for the past two or three decades. The treatment rests on that long-term relationship, not on the fear of death.

One of the most effective ways of persuading the members of a small congregation to enter into a cooperative arrangement for ministerial services is to offer the choice of "cooperate or disband."

One of the most persuasive approaches for presenting the alternative of a bivocational minister is to emphasize the possibility of a long-term relationship with this person. Occasionally this is expressed in this question to an older policy maker of the small church: "When you die, who do you want to officiate at your funeral? A minister who specializes in funerals, but a person you view as a distant acquaintance? Or a person who has been your pastor for several years and someone you regard as a longtime friend as well as your pastor?"

A Central Question

What should the small church place at the top of the priority list? Should it increase the degree of cooperation with other congregations in doing ministry? Should it participate in a joint vacation Bible school, in union Thanksgiving services, in a shared ministry with youth or with single adults or with senior citizens or with childless couples? Should it run its own after-school program or join in a cooperative effort with three other churches? Should it share a minister with one or more other congregations? Or choose a bivocational pastoral team who will relate only to that one congregation?

The answer, as it is with so many other complex questions, is that it depends.

If the goal is to strengthen ties with other congregations, the cooperative path is the road to follow.

If the top priority is to offer a community witness that churches do believe in cooperation and joint programming, that obviously means cooperate!

If the number-one goal is to respond to complaints, "There are too few of us to do that," one alternative is to seek to build a viable group by joint programming.

If there is broad-based support for numerical growth, and if the local setting makes that appear to be a reasonable goal, then the best advice is to ignore opportunities for interchurch cooperation in what are usually seen as congregational ministries (in contrast to social welfare and advocacy ministries). Instead, concentrate on matching the local competition in quality; in publicity; in creating additional entry points for newcomers to welcoming places in your fellowship; in identifying and responding to the religious agendas of skeptics, pilgrims, searchers, agnostics, seekers, and others on a religious quest; in serious and in-depth Bible study; in the ministry of music; and in the proclamation of the gospel.

If most of the leaders are convinced that institutional survival goals should be at the top of the local agenda, it may be appropriate to study interchurch cooperation as a road to survival. (**Caution:** Institutional survival goals rarely attract new members.) If, for example, your denomination has ruled that only fully credentialed ministers may serve Holy Communion, a cooperative arrangement in staffing may be the only way your congregation can offer the Lord's Supper every Sunday morning. That may be the only way to secure the weekly services of a fully credentialed pastor.

Is Denial a Motivating Force?

In many urban communities, a primary motivating factor behind intercongregational cooperation is an unwillingness to accept the fact that small congregations cannot function effectively as miniature models of large churches. Instead of carving out a distinctive identity and niche, the decision is to cooperate with other small churches and copy the programming of large congregations.

In rural America, support for a cooperative ministry may be based on the dream that will be a means to perpetuate yesterday, at least for a few more years. Instead of recognizing the need for change, a cooperative arrangement often promises that yesterday is a viable model for tomorrow.

The realists in each setting will recognize that denial is not a source of either hope or creativity.

Is Cooperation an Alternative to Competition?

In several hundred rural counties in the United States, cooperation in ministry is seen as a method for gaining greater productivity from limited resources. The most common expression of this is when two or more congregations, no one of which can either afford or justify a full-time and fully credentialed pastor, join together to provide the compensation for one minister who will serve all of the participating congregations. This usually means that these congregations do not expect to be able to compete with the larger congregations with a full-scale program meeting in a building five to fifteen miles away. Thirty years later, it is clear to at least a few that cooperation can be a means of reducing competition among the churches. Where once three congregations from the same or similar religious traditions competed with one another for members, only one of those three congregations remains.

Frequently that cooperation is really an illusion, however, since two new congregations representing other religious traditions have been founded in that community.

Occasionally, a powerful motivating factor in both rural and urban areas has been to create a model of ministry that resembles the large urban congregations. This model usually calls for greater specialization of skills and labor for the paid staff, a more sophisticated approach to the corporate worship of God, more extensive programming, and an increase in joint ministries. It is a first cousin to what the progressive reformers advocated in the early decades of the twentieth century. Thus it may also encourage the consolidation of seven or eight self-governing congregations into two or three. If that is the long-term goal of this strategy, it probably will be achieved.

The Big Risks

Many, many years ago, most of the leaders in the foreign missions movement agreed that it was necessary to minimize the danger of colonialism or dependency on the missionary from another culture as soon as feasible. New congregations organized by missionaries would display these four characteristics: They would be self-governing, self-financing, self-expressing, and self-propagating.

These also are characteristics of healthy churches in North American Protestantism. One way to undermine that new mission is to extend the financial subsidy for longer than two or three years. One way to undermine that small congregation founded back in 1897 is to offer generous financial subsidies in return for joining a multichurch parish. Another is to minimize the self-governing or self-expressing facets of congregational life.

A common risk surfaces with the most successful multichurch parishes that offer an extensive parish-centered package of ministries. These can become attractive entry points for newcomers who soon identify with the parish as a whole, rather than with one of the participating congregations. This dilutes the distinctive identity of each of the participating congregations and undermines their efforts at self-propagation. If the long-term goal is the eventual consolidation of these four or five or six or seven small congregations into one legal entity, perhaps with two or three or four meeting places, eroding these four characteristics of each participating congregation often can be an effective means for achieving that goal.

Four Concluding Comments

Four comments summarize this discussion.

First, the erosion of denominational loyalties means that today small churches are not only competing with other congregations within their denomination, but that most also are competing for replacement members with churches from a growing variety of religious traditions. The competition among the churches today for adults born after 1955 is far greater than it was in earlier decades for prospective new members born before 1940.

Second, cooperative arrangements among congregations in a Christian witness, in social welfare ministries, in missions, in leadership training, in advocacy on public policy issues, and in founding new religious institutions can be creative, healthy, and productive.

Third, intercongregational cooperation in parish ministries (worship, teaching, music, staffing, youth programming, etc.) and numerical growth usually turn out to be mutually incompatible goals.

Finally, the record of the twentieth century clearly demonstrates that if the driving goal is the consolidation of small churches, intercongregational cooperation in local ministries can be an effective road to reach that goal.

4.

SEVEN FORKS IN THE ROAD INTO THE THIRD MILLENNIUM

What will the twenty-first century bring to the small Protestant congregation that averages fewer than seventy-five to a hundred people at worship? One answer comes in four parts.

Perhaps 10 to 15 percent of the small churches of today will have their future determined by external forces. The population of that rural county in the Great Plains continues to grow older and fewer in numbers. In the Southeast or in the Mississippi River Valley, a tornado or hurricane or fire or flood destroys the building. Instead of rebuilding, the members decide to disband or to merge with another congregation. The small English-speaking Anglo congregation in Los Angeles or Detroit finds it cannot reach the newcomers moving into that neighborhood, and so it narrows its options to merger, relocation, or dissolution. After twelve years the denomination terminates the financial subsidy for a central-city mission. By that time this small church has become so dependent on the subsidy that it concludes merger or disbanding are the only options left.

In a few religious traditions, denominational policies will urge certain small churches to merge or to relocate the meeting place or to enter into a cooperative arrangement with one or more other congregations. The success or failure of those denominational policies will determine the future of perhaps 5 percent of small Protestant congregations during the next two decades.

Another 5 to 10 percent of today's small churches will decide that their future lies with an administrative merger with a large "missionary church." Title to the property is conveyed to the missionary church with a clear understanding that the small church's building will continue to be the meeting place for a worshiping community for at least seven years. The merger agreement calls for one budget, one staff, one governing board, and two or three meeting places for the newly merged congregation.

What happens next? The historical record of these experiences suggests that some of these small churches are really "wounded birds" that, with proper care, will be able to fly again. One example is the new mission that peaked in size with over a hundred members but, after two or three demoralizing pastorates, was ready to close. Instead of closing, this wounded bird is adopted by the missionary church. After it recovers, it flies alone as an autonomous and healthy church.[1] Another example is the hundred-year-old ex-rural parish that is overwhelmed by suburbanization. Instead of growing older and smaller, it is adopted by the missionary church, which provides the leadership required to transform it into a healthy and growing suburban parish able to respond to the religious agendas of new generations.

In other situations, after five or six funerals, the members of that wounded bird congregation decide to take the final step and become part of the community that worships at the missionary church's meeting place.

Others are helped to define a new role with a new non-Anglo constituency and, with the guidance of new leadership, to accept and fulfill that new role. For at least 5 percent and perhaps for as many as 10 percent of today's small congregations, this temporary adoption by a self-identified missionary church is a far more attractive option than disbanding or merging with another small congregation.

What about the other 65 to 75 percent? What will the third millennium bring to them? Most will take one of seven forks in the road into the twenty-first century. What are those forks in that road?

The Downhill Path

The easiest path into the twenty-first century, and for many people the most attractive because it is the easiest, is to avoid making decisions and simply to drift along into tomorrow. Given the demographic context of contemporary North America, for most this will mean passively watching as the members grow older in age and fewer in numbers. At each well-attended funeral, a growing number of the mourners will silently speculate, "I wonder who will be next." Individual and institutional survival top the list of local concerns.

A slightly different version of this course of action can be identified by the answer to these questions: Who are the folks your congregation is seeking to reach? What are the characteristics of the people your congregation is best prepared to reach and serve? The goalless congregation that is drifting into tomorrow usually answers that question in these terms, "Everyone. We welcome everyone who desires to join us." This response may come from the three-year-old, struggling new mission, or it may come from the formerly prosperous suburban parish that has shrunk from an average of three hundred people at worship to fewer than ninety today. If you do not know where you are going, any road will take you there.

The 180 Degree Choice

The sharpest fork in the road ahead of the small church was described in the first chapter. Do we want to be a healthy second-commandment congregation that places at the top of the agenda the quality of the relationships among our people? Or do we want to transform ourselves into primarily a first-commandment church that concentrates first of all on identifying and offering a meaningful response to the religious needs of people we have yet to meet?

The temptation, of course, is to reply, "Both." Unfortunately, however, it is a rare small congregation that is able to mobilize the resources needed for two top priorities.

The best of the small churches that affirm and fulfill their primary role as second-commandment churches can remain on a plateau in size far into the third millennium. Most of those congregations who accept that role, but do not work at fulfilling it by also at least a passable effort at meeting the religious needs of their people, will find themselves growing older and smaller in the early years of the twenty-first century.

Those congregations who successfully transform themselves into primarily first-commandment churches with very high quality ministries will grow larger in number and younger in the age of their constituency. Those who attempt that transformation, but fail to successfully implement that goal, may find themselves torn by internal conflict over identity and role.

How Large Is the Circle?

For at least one-third of all small churches, the road into the third millennium will be symbolized by the size of their parking lot. One group of congregational leaders is convinced that the privately owned automobile is a central component of the American culture. They will redefine the service area of their congregation as a circle with a radius of ten to thirty minutes in travel time on Sunday morning. If they can reinforce that worldview with either a healthy second-commandment role or a high-quality, first-commandment role, the institutional survival of that congregation is guaranteed far into the twenty-first century.

Many more congregational leaders will decide that the top priority should be reaching, attracting, serving, assimilating, and discipling residents who live within walking distance of the meeting place. They will draw a small circle on the map to define that church's service area. If they succeed in implementing that fivefold strategy, their best days are ahead of them. Usually the leaders find their greatest frustration is in identifying models that have made that fivefold strategy work in a small geographical circle of residents. Where do we turn to find success stories of this model that we can study? (This is the first alternative offered in chapter 5.)

Is It Really a Competitive World?

A fourth fork in the road into the twenty-first century was described in chapter 3. This is a judgment call. What is the most accurate description of contemporary reality in today's ecclesiastical world? Were the urban-based progressive reformers of the first half of the twentieth century right? Is interchurch cooperation the most promising road for congregations to choose as they move into the third millennium?

Or is it an increasingly competitive world in which that rapidly growing number of church shoppers has forced the churches to compete with one another for new generations of replacement members? Has the erosion of institutional loyalties, both congregational and denominational, been a source or a by-product of this enhanced competition? Or is the increased intercongregational competition, both across and within denominational lines, largely a product of the escalating demand for quality?

Or is intercongregational cooperation the best way to combat competition? Or is intercongregational cooperation the best road for smaller congregations, who either cannot or will not compete on quality, to take into the twenty-first century?

This is a judgment call that every Protestant congregation, regardless of size or religious tradition, will have to make on its way into the third millennium.

Who Is the Enemy?

A most provocative question has been raised by Professor Robert Wuthnow. In his reflections on the challenges ahead for the churches, Wuthnow has written that "liberalism needs to become a counterculture to secularism, instead of a reaction to fundamentalism."[2] This is a powerful insight that deserves careful consideration by leaders of small Protestant congregations located toward the liberal end of the theological spectrum.

The magnetic personality can rally a large following by identifying an enemy and mobilizing the followers to hate that enemy. Their identity is in who or what they oppose. That can be no more than a temporary role for a Christian church. One reason is that Jesus told his followers to love their enemies. A second reason is that on a long-term basis, institutions do better by building their identity on who they are, what they support, and what they do, not on opposition to an enemy or who they are not.

The most productive road for all churches to take into the third millennium is to turn to another quotation from Wuthnow in a different context and to be "devoted to the ideals of service, caring for the poor and disadvantaged, promoting community, reconciliation, and the transmission of values through teaching and training the young."[3] That, incidentally, is what Professor Wuthnow hopefully projects as the future of the religious right.

Which path will your congregation choose to follow? Organizing against an enemy? Or clarifying what it stands for and concentrating on what it does best in ministry?

Follow the Leader

For many congregational leaders, the most attractive scenario is to find the pastor who brings in one body a magnetic personality, transformational leadership skills, inspiring preaching, a compelling vision of what God is calling this congregation to be and to do, a high Christology, a deep Christian commitment, and a productive work ethic.

When that new pastor points to the future and calls out, "Follow me!" everyone eagerly and enthusiastically falls into line. That new pastor accepts the responsibility for choosing the best path for this congregation to follow into tomorrow.

With only three reservations, this is an enticing alternative for the small church. One reservation is the severe national shortage of leaders with all of these qualities. A second is that they tend to prefer large congregations over small churches. The third, and the most serious reservation, is that most small congregations have failed to create a congregational culture that is compatible with this leadership style. That style of pastoral leadership is more appropriate for the self-identified first-commandment church than for most second-commandment congregations.

Who Is Our Constituency?

The seventh fork in that road into the third millennium raises a question that is disturbing to many, but completely acceptable to others.

Those who find it most disturbing are Christians who are convinced that Paul's admonition to "become all things to all people" (1 Cor. 9:22) applies to every congregation and means that every congregation should seek to reach and save everyone with no exceptions. This interpretation of Scripture means that no congregation is free to target a specific audience.

On the other hand, others interpret this and similar passages to mean that the universal church has an obligation to seek to reach and to save every living person on this planet. No one congregation, however, is obligated to be all things to all people nor to preach the gospel every week in several hundred languages nor to expect to be able to respond effectively to all the religious needs of every individual. This second interpretation affirms that other Christian congregations are legitimate orders of God's creation.

This second interpretation also undergirds the assumption that no one congregation can reach and serve everyone. Therefore, who are the people your church will seek to reach, serve, and challenge? What are the characteristics of the people your congregation will be serving ten years hence?

The second-commandment church begins to answer that question with these words: "First of all, of course, our members. Second, their kinfolk, including their children, their friends, their neighbors, their colleagues at work, and others they may invite to join us."

By contrast, the evangelistic first-commandment congregation may begin to answer that question with these words: "First of all, the people who are comfortable in the language we speak, who do not have any active church affiliation, who display at least a minimal degree of interest in hearing how the gospel of Jesus Christ speaks to their lives and their concerns, and who . . . "

The most highly visible example of this distinction can be seen in the newspaper advertisements placed by churches. Frequently the second-commandment congregations will design an ad that resembles the "tombstone" ads found in the financial pages of the *Wall Street Journal* or *The New York Times*. A brokerage firm uses these ads to announce a new issue of common stock or bonds. The ad includes the name, address, and telephone number of the firm and a brief description of the amount of that stock or bond issue. It also advises that this is simply an announcement, not an invitation to purchase.

The parallel box designed by these second-commandment churches carries the name of the congregation, the denominational affiliation (often in much smaller type), the address, a telephone number, the name of the pastor, and the Sunday schedule. A few also list the text and the title of next Sunday's sermon and/or carry a short slogan or a logo.

It appears that the primary audiences for these tombstone ads are (1) local clergy, (2) leaders from the advertising church who are glad to see that their congregation is advertising, (3) newcomers to the community who are looking for a church of their tradition, (4) newcomers who are committed churchgoers and who are shopping churches from several traditions, (5) inactive members of that congregation who check the church ads every week to be sure their church has not closed, and (6) visiting clergy who like to read church advertisements.

In business jargon, these ads are designed to "push the product" of the church that designed the ad. These are sales ads, not marketing efforts.[4]

The first-commandment church is far more likely to follow a marketing strategy. That means designing a newspaper ad that focuses on the agenda of the reader, rather than on the agenda of the producer of the ad.

Before these ads can be designed, two questions must be answered. First, what does this church do best? What is our number-one point of excellence? What do we have to offer? Second, what are the characteristics of the people whom we are seeking to reach with our ad?

One church with a superb six-day-a-week ministry with children runs ads that include photographs of smiling children. Above each smiling face is a brief quotation about why that child is happy to be involved in that church's program. Another church with an extensive recreation/small-group ministry designed for young, never-married adults advertises on the Monday sports pages of the local newspaper. A third congregation is led by a preacher who excels in sermons that bring the power of the gospel to problems many adults confront in their daily life. Instead of advertising the text and sermon, each weekly newspaper ad consists of a photograph depicting two people in a brief discussion of that problem. Below the photograph are the words that advise the reader that will be the topic of next Sunday's sermon.

These newspaper advertisements do not represent a sales program that begins with the advertiser's product, but a marketing effort that begins with the needs of the consumer.

The fork-in-the-road question for the policy makers in the small church is symbolized by the contrast between these two approaches to newspaper ads: Will we carefully and precisely define our future constituency, seek to identify their religious needs, and respond to those needs? Or will we welcome everyone who comes and attempt to redefine our ministry to fulfill the needs of whoever may come?

Will we be reactive? Or will we be proactive?

These seven forks in the road constitute one of the central themes of this book. At least two-thirds, and perhaps as many as three-fourths of the small churches of today have a far broader array of choices open to them than most of their leaders realize. This can be illustrated by reviewing 44 of the alternatives. The length of this list supports the contention that the self-fulfilling prophecy is available to most small congregations.

5.

44 SCENARIOS FOR TOMORROW

I wonder if our church will be open a year from now,"
questioned the fifty-four-year-old Harold Brown, who
had married into the Maple Grove Church thirty years
earlier. "The way things are going around here, this
doesn't seem to be a healthy time for small churches. My
cousin told me a week ago that their church was going to
merge with another small congregation in August, and the
church my brother and his wife joined in Chicago back in
1958 just closed. It doesn't seem to matter whether you're
talking about the big cities or rural communities like this;
every small institution is being crowded out by the big ones.
You can see it happening with drugstores, public schools,
filling stations, doctors' offices, grocery stores, and movie
theaters as well as churches."

"I've been wondering about that, too," added sixty-year-old
Thelma Green. "What's the future for small churches like
ours?"

"Do you two expect to be alive a year from today?" asked the
denominational representative who was meeting with Harold,
Thelma, and three other leaders from the 117-year-old Maple

Grove Church. This was the first of what had been scheduled as three meetings to plan the next steps following the retirement in four months of the sixty-nine-year-old part-time pastor.

"I sure hope so!" replied Harold.

"Unless you know something about me that I don't know, I certainly expect to be alive a year from now!" declared Thelma. "Why do you ask?"

"Two reasons," replied the visitor. "First, the annual death rate for small churches like this one is exactly the same as it is for fifty-four-year-old white men and sixty-year-old white women. It is 0.8 percent per year. For each one of you two, the chances of being alive a year from now are slightly better than ninety-nine out of a hundred. Likewise, the chances are slightly better than ninety-nine out of a hundred that the typical small Protestant church also will be alive one year from now.

"The second reason I bring it up is that the future looks brighter for this congregation than it does for either of you two. Twenty years from now, Harold, when you are seventy-four, the chances of your surviving for one more year probably will be down to about ninety-five out of a hundred and for Thelma it also will be about ninety-five out of a hundred, but for this congregation it will continue to be about ninety-nine out of a hundred."

"You mean that when I'm eighty, my chances of dying in the next twelve months are only five out of a hundred?" challenged Thelma.

"Yep," replied the visitor, "if you make it to eighty, and at your age, the chances are better than two-out-of-three that you will, the chances are approximately nineteen out of twenty that you'll survive another twelve months. That's why the Social Security trust fund will be running into trouble. You folks are living too long."

"How about me?" inquired Harold.

"Well, the chances of a fifty-four-year-old white male surviving for another twenty years aren't quite as good as for the sixty-year-old white female, but if you make it to seventy-four, you will have nineteen out of twenty chances to celebrate your seventy-fifth birthday."[1]

"This is all very interesting, and I'm delighted to learn that we can expect Thelma and Harold to be with us for at least twenty more years, but what's that got to do with how we replace Reverend Harrison, who will be retiring in four months?" interrupted a third member of the group.

"First, I don't believe you should be alarmed about the future of this congregation," explained the denominational staff person. "Small churches are tough. They are not fragile institutions. Reverend and Mrs. Harrison came here four years ago when he retired from the full-time ministry. My impression is that he has done a good job here. You were averaging about eighty at worship when he came, and last year you averaged about eighty-five. If you want, I believe we can help you find another semiretired minister to succeed Reverend Harrison. You have an excellent parsonage, and you pay slightly over half of what we define as minimum salary for a full-time pastor plus utilities, health insurance, and pension. You really don't have anything to worry about.

"Second, while I would encourage you to do some careful planning for the future of Maple Grove Church, you're under no pressure. The growth of the tourist, recreational, and retirement slices of the local economy suggest that you could expand your ministries, but no one can force you to do that. That's up to you. I'm convinced that you could double in size in ten years if you wanted to, but no one is going to force you to change. You may want to consider looking for a younger full-time pastor who could help you grow, but that is up to you."

"What do you think we ought to do?" asked Harold Brown. "You have a lot more experience than we do. Do you recommend we look for another semiretired pastor like Reverend Harrison?

91

Or do you think we should look for a young and energetic minister who would come and stay for ten or fifteen years and lead us in creating a new future?"

"First of all, it's not my job to tell you what you should do," declared this representative from the regional denominational judicatory. "That's your decision. You will have to live with the consequences, so that should be your decision."

"Well, what do you think should be our next step?" inquired Thelma Green.

"That's my point," came the reply. "I suggest you do two things. First, draw up a list of alternative scenarios for the future of the Maple Grove Church. You are larger and stronger than most of our small churches, and your location also expands your range of choices. I believe it would be easy to list at least twenty different scenarios for the future of this church. If you wish, we can begin to build that list this evening.

"Next, I would suggest you begin to identify the criteria that you could use to evaluate each scenario. Rather than use the personal preferences of your leaders to choose from among these alternative scenarios, identify the criteria to use in sorting these out."

"I'm afraid you lost me somewhere along the way," interrupted Harold. "I understand what you mean by choices among various scenarios, but can you give me an example of what you mean by criteria?"

"Sure," was the instant reply. "For example, today most of your people come from within a five-mile radius. Are you willing to try to expand that to a service area with a radius of seven to ten miles? You have an exceptionally well-maintained building here, but exclusive of the cemetery, you have only slightly over an acre of land. Are you open to making a fresh start at a new location on a larger site? When I worshiped here with you a few months ago, I noticed that I was one of the youngest adults in the room, and I will be forty-seven next month. Are you willing to make the changes necessary to reach younger generations?

Would you be willing to purchase the house next door that has a 'For Sale' sign in front of it and level the house in order to provide more off-street parking? Your primary focus in ministry is now on taking care of your present members, and I can understand why that is true. Would you be willing to make that the second priority in ministry? Those are five examples of criteria. If each one of those is a controlling factor in your decision making, that will make it easy to cut your list of twenty or more scenarios down to three or four or five. I would strongly suggest, however, that we not look at criteria now. The first step is to build that list of alternative scenarios. We can begin that tonight and complete it at our next meeting. After all of your members have had a chance to discuss those scenarios, and perhaps add to that list, we can build the list of criteria. That could be at the third meeting we have scheduled. If you want me to come back after that for one or more additional meetings, I will be glad to. That's my job, to help congregations like this one in their planning for a new era."

Seven Insights

This conversation illustrates seven important considerations in planning for the future of the small Protestant congregation in North America. First, small churches are tough. They have a long life expectancy. Relatively few die or merge or dissolve in any given year.

Second, most small congregations have many more options open to them than the members believe to be true. Most do not have as many highly attractive alternative futures open to them as are before the leaders at the Maple Grove Church, but it usually is easy to build a list of eight to fifteen alternative scenarios.

Third, and perhaps most important for this discussion, the Maple Grove Church is an excellent example of a healthy, vital, faithful, and institutionally strong second-commandment congregation.

Fourth, like many self-identified, small second-commandment congregations, the Maple Grove Church is close to a participatory democracy in terms of governance. This denominational staffer wisely recognizes that (a) that is the system here; (b) the stronger the orientation toward participatory democracy, the greater the resistance to change; and (c) the smaller the number of members, the more important it is to broaden the participation base. If this were a ten-year-old congregation averaging eight hundred at worship and still led by the founding pastor, it probably would be both possible and appropriate for that outside interventionist to meet with the senior pastor, one other key program staff person, and four or five of the most influential volunteer leaders. In a few hours, or in two meetings at the most, that small group could decide on a strategy for the next two or three years and map out the first several steps to turn that dream into reality.

The number-one learning about participatory democracy over the past four decades is disturbing to many. The only way to persuade everyone that her or his opinion is valuable and cannot be ignored is to grant everyone the power of veto. The one thing that cannot be vetoed is the status quo.[2] As a result, participatory democracy has turned out to be the one form of congregational self-government that is most resistant to change. Since many small congregations view themselves as participatory democracies with every member's vote equal in weight to the vote of any other member, it is predictable that small churches will be more resistant to innovation than are larger congregations that rely on a system of representative church government or those very large congregations that are governed by a relatively small elite.

This particular denominational staffer understands that distinction and is not about to yield to the pleas to tell the people at the Maple Grove Church what they should do. This staff person also understands that seven of the variables needed to make a participatory democracy work effectively are (1) time; (2) patience; (3) choices; (4) giving everyone the opportunity to speak, to be heard, and to become convinced they have been heard;[3] (5) trust; (6) more talk; and (7) more time for people to be able to talk themselves into supporting what they initially opposed. This staffer expects and is willing to participate as an outside interventionist in at least four or five subsequent meetings at the Maple Grove Church.

Fifth, the Maple Grove Church also illustrates the point that one of the most promising openings for outside intervention is in the months before the end of a pastorate of a widely appreciated and greatly loved minister.

Sixth, this conversation illustrates the value of an outside third party in stimulating thinking, injecting new insights, suggesting alternatives, and building on strengths.

Finally, this conversation introduces one three-step planning model. That model consists of (a) building a list of alternative courses of action or scenarios for the future, (b) defining the criteria that will be used to choose from among those scenarios, and (c) choosing a course of action and implementing it. This planning model is biased toward maximizing continuity with the past because most scenarios begin with the view from today's reality. Later in this chapter, another three-step planning model will be described that is more compatible with radical change.

This conversation also introduces several of the alternatives open to many small churches, but before expanding that list, it may be useful to examine four other issues.

What Will Be the Process?

The choice of the model for planning ranks second only to the choice of the criteria for selecting members of a long-range planning committee in influencing the results of any effort to plan for a new day. Scores of planning models are available. One three-step model that begins with building a list of potential scenarios was described earlier. A widely used planning process is to begin by listing all the problems confronting that congregation. That model often leads to despair. Perhaps the most widely followed planning model in American Protestantism is to focus on money and use the budgeting process as the vehicle for making planning decisions. Another is to use a church-growth model.

A popular planning model begins with the definition of a statement of purpose or mission. The second step calls for the definition of broad general objectives. One such objective might be to accept the role as a regional church. Another might be to seek to become a multicultural parish. Or a different objective might be to reach young never-married adults. The third step consists of formulating the specific, attainable, and measurable goals required to turn those general objectives into reality.

This model works best with a centralized decision-making process, a long-tenured pastor who is a strong leader, a relatively small governing board of five to nine members, and a willingness to focus on a narrowly defined constituency. It rarely is a useful model if the goal is to become a highly pluralistic congregation or when much of the authority for decision making is spread among several standing committees such as personnel, property, finances, and missions.

One of the most widely used and less threatening planning models is to begin by identifying strengths, assets, and resources and examining how those can become the foundation for launching new ministries. The second step requires an examination of what the competition is for each alternative course of action. The third step is to choose between competing directly with the specialties of one or more churches or to carve out a distinctive niche in ministry. Market-driven leaders usually are most comfortable with this model.[4]

44 Scenarios for Tomorrow

A challenging planning model for most, but not all, small congregations is one that consists of three sets of questions. It is simple to describe, easy to follow, and supportive of radical change. Instead of beginning with an examination of the status quo or seeking to respond to a crisis or using last year's expenditures as a beginning point, this model is based on the assumption that God has a place for every congregation in God's world. Thus the first question is obvious.

1. What is the Lord calling our church to be and to do in the years ahead? Instead of seeking to perpetuate yesterday, let us prayerfully seek God's direction. This step is in response to a bit of wisdom from *Alice's Adventures in Wonderland*. If you do not know where you are going, any road will take you there. Sometimes this first step is described as defining a vision for tomorrow.

2. What is contemporary reality? What is our beginning point as we step into tomorrow? Another bit of ancient wisdom advises that you cannot get there from here unless you know where here is.

3. How do we get from here to there? What changes will be required to turn that vision of a new tomorrow into reality?

This is sometimes described as the vision model for planning. Effective implementation requires (1) a pastor who is an exceptionally competent agent of planned change initiated from within an organization and (2) broad-based support for radical change. This is an excellent planning model if the goal is to double in size in a decade or to relocate the meeting place or to change from growing older and smaller to growing younger and larger. It is not the best model if the goal is only modest change.

Why Will This Process Not Work for Everyone?

This vision-centered planning model does not work in perhaps one-third of all North American Protestant congregations, regardless of size or denominational identity. Why? The answer can be summarized in five words: An absence of widespread discontent. Most of the members, with perhaps the exception of three or four knowledgeable leaders, are convinced that all is well. To be more precise, there is an absence of discontent with the status quo, which means that no one will be motivated to initiate change. Discontent is the essential foundation for planned change initiated from within any organization.[5]

Why is there an absence of discontent? In some congregations the explanation is obvious. Everyone is happy with how things are going now. This does not mean that change is not necessary. All it means is that no one is eager to initiate change.

A second, and perhaps more common, explanation is denial. Many congregations are in a state of denial. One example is the severely fragmented congregation that was torn apart by a pastor who excelled in polarizing the membership. After three or four years of shrinking numbers, that pastor departs. The successor is a warm, loving, caring, extroverted, charming, exceptionally productive, and attractive shepherd. Within several months, worship attendance begins to climb. Former opponents in the previous battles rebuild their friendship ties. The second most accurate word to describe the new reality is *euphoria*. A better word, however, is *drifting*. That congregation continues to be a purposeless and goalless institution that now is drifting happily into tomorrow. If someone suggests that new goals need to be formulated, that proposal is met with denial. "We are so relieved that yesteryear is behind us that we simply want to relax and enjoy the absence of divisive conflict."

At the other end of the spectrum is the congregation in which nearly everyone is convinced that next year will be 1957 and the only challenge is to do yesterday over again, only better.

A crucial component of that three-step vision-planning model described earlier is an accurate description of contemporary reality. When denial is substituted for that second step, the process will not be productive. At least a couple of the leaders need to renew their curiosity about tomorrow, to dig below the surface to identify what is really happening, and to speak the truth about what they see. Truth is the best antidote for denial.[6] Who will speak that truth? The long-tenured pastor nearing retirement or the new minister who engendered that feeling of euphoria may not be in the best position to send that message.

It also should be emphasized that this planning model will not work in the absence of skilled agents of planned change initiated from within an organization. That skill, however, can be taught and learned.

Who Are the Exceptions?

A third word of caution about that three-step vision model applies to perhaps another 10 percent of today's churches. These include (a) those congregations in which the internal conflict between the pastor and the leaders dominates the agenda; (b) denominationally affiliated congregations in which a highly divisive issue not only dominates the agenda of that regional judicatory and/or the national denomination, but now has forced congregational leaders to choose up sides (examples include abortion as an approved form of birth control, the ordination of homosexuals, the financial support of the denominational budget, foreign policy, or civil liberties); (c) parishes in which an influential pastor is looking forward to retirement a few years hence and forbids any planning for a new era until after that retirement day; (d) congregations with a severe shortage of future-oriented leaders; (e) churches in which institutional survival dominates the current agenda; (f) parishes that have been receiving substantial annual financial subsidies from the income from endowment funds or from bequests or from denominational sources; or (g) churches that have changed pastors three or four times during the past decade and are perfecting their skills at welcoming and working with a new pastor; or (h) congregations in which few, if any, of the volunteer leaders have a thorough knowledge of the facts reflecting contemporary reality.

Where Do We Begin?

While less common than it was forty years ago, in a fair number of Protestant congregations, an early item on the "business agenda" at the monthly meeting of the governing board is the treasurer's report. This often influences the context of all subsequent discussions. Money, rather than ministry and mission, becomes the most influential factor in policy making. The best that can be said for this is that it is compatible with the use of the budget as the heart of the planning model.

This beginning with the treasurer's report also illustrates the point that the choice of a beginning point often turns out to be a highly influential factor in what happens later. Thus some governing boards schedule the treasurer's report as their last item on the agenda of that monthly meeting. Others replace the oral report with a printed report that is distributed for informational purposes.

The balance of this chapter suggests 44 different courses of action for leaders as they seek to shape the future for their church. These alternatives are presented under six different headings. The most productive results probably will come if identifying a future constituency is the beginning point for the discussion. The three-step planning process described earlier can be a useful format to follow in seeking to identify a future constituency.

The least productive results are likely to come from two other beginning points. One is to focus on institutional survival goals. The other is to begin by examining alternatives for providing fully credentialed pastoral leadership for that small church.

It may not be a coincidence that the positive, but challenging alternatives outnumber the institutional survival and staffing alternatives in this chapter by a three-to-one ratio. Unfortunately, some readers may find the institutional survival and staffing alternatives to be both more attractive and easier beginning points in preparing for a new tomorrow.

Producer or Consumer?

The longest, the most challenging, and potentially the most productive list of alternatives for small churches also requires the most radical changes in perspective. That is one reason for choosing a planning model that is compatible with and supportive of radical change if the decision is to pick an alternative from this first of sixteen possibilities.

This point can be illustrated by this remark: "I can't understand why more people don't come to our church. The folks here are the friendliest group of people I've ever met. We have a nice minister who is a good speaker; we have a good Sunday school for children with several really dedicated teachers. Our choir is not the best in the world, but they enjoy singing. We have a good building, and the fellowship hall and kitchen were completely remodeled only a few years ago. We don't have any debt, and there must be a thousand people who live within a couple of miles of our church. At least a third of them don't go to church anywhere. I can't understand why our numbers keep going down."

One response to that concern is that it is the end of the twentieth century, not the middle of it. A better answer is that it is easier to shrink in size than to grow. The best response is in the content of the statement. That comment describes what that congregation has to offer. It ignores both the wants and the needs of those people who might be potential new members in the future.

While many people resent this trend, one fact of contemporary life is the consumer orientation of society. In business this is described as focusing on the needs of the customer. Once upon a time a business was able to produce a high quality product that would sell itself. During the past several decades, however, the world has changed. Many businesses have gone bankrupt because they concentrated on producing a product that the consumers did not want.

In the 1950s the emphasis was on sales. That meant "pushing your product." More recently that emphasis on sales has been replaced by marketing. In marketing the beginning point is on the needs of the customer, not on the product.[7]

"We have a wonderful Sunday school; I wonder why more parents aren't sending their children to our Sunday school." That is a sales question. A marketing approach would begin with a question such as this: "What are the needs of today's parents and their children that we could meet in our Sunday school?" Instead of beginning with the services or product the institution offers, this approach begins with the needs of the people. For example, Jesus repeatedly began conversations with individuals by asking, "Where do you hurt?"

The alternatives presented in this first group of possible scenarios for small churches share one point of commonality. All sixteen alternatives focus on the identification of a new constituency. All sixteen are based on the same five basic assumptions.

1. Sooner or later all of the present members of this small congregation will die, drop out, or move away.

2. Most of their children will not be members of this congregation in the year 2025.

3. It is difficult, and also pointless, for a church to continue without people.

4. The best time to begin to identify tomorrow's constituency is today.

5. Most important, all sixteen of these alternative courses of action are based on the assumption that this congregation can and will begin planning on the basis of responding to the religious and personal needs of people rather than on what that parish offers. If that is unacceptable or impossible, it may be wise to

skip this section and to look at the alternatives under leadership and programming.

What Are the Options?

1. Establish or reestablish the primary role as a neighborhood church. Identify the people who live within a mile or two of the building as the primary constituency for tomorrow.

This is the most difficult to implement of any of these sixteen alternatives. Few churches have been able to do it. It can be done, however, and it is being done. Implementation of this strategy requires patience, persistence, hard work, repeated calling door to door, a genuine sensitivity to the needs of people, love, creativity, and lots of listening.

The typical strategy includes (a) making the church building the center of community life; (b) scheduling at least eight or ten events annually at the church that are designed to meet the needs of nearby residents; (c) knocking on every door ("I'm here simply to get acquainted" or "I dropped by to invite you to this special event next month") at least four times annually; (d) an excellent adult teaching ministry; (e) a genuine commitment to the goal of becoming a neighborhood church; (f) a worship service on Sunday morning that a complete stranger to that religious tradition will find easy to share in as well as a meaningful experience; (g) door-to-door, and whenever possible face-to-face, delivery of the invitations to attend the special events, programs, and services at that church; and (h) a long pastorate by an extroverted and personable minister, since much of the continuity will be in the person of that pastor.

This strategy is consistent with a role as a second-commandment church that is both a great good third place and a "Cheers" model of relationships.

This alternative is easier to implement if most of the nearby residents live in structures that house one to four families than if the building is located in a commercial district or in a high-rise apartment neighborhood.

2. Become a regional church for a narrowly and precisely defined constituency. In geographical terms, this is at the other end of the spectrum. Instead of seeking to reach and serve a relatively large proportion of the people living near the congregation's meeting place, the focus here is on a tiny proportion of the residents of a large geographical area.

One example is the congregation designed for totally deaf and other hearing-impaired adults. Less visible are the congregations designed to serve (a) adults in their second or subsequent marriage; (b) Cantonese-speaking recent immigrants from China; (c) never-married professional and businesswomen who have chosen to become mothers; (d) people who seek a church in which the worship experience is built around drama, contemporary music, and a high level of participation by the congregation; (e) parents who seek a bilingual nursery school for their children; (f) never-married adults in the 19-25 age bracket; (g) single fathers; (h) parents who are educating their children at home; (i) adults on a serious religious pilgrimage who seek a church that addresses the questions of agnostics, searchers, seekers, pilgrims, and the curious; (j) parents who seek a church with an excellent ministry with families that include teenagers; (k) self-identified charismatic Christians; (l) adults who prefer a church that projects very high expectations of those seeking to become members; (m) parents of children with serious physical disabilities; or (n) people looking for exceptionally high-quality preaching.

That is far from a complete list! The point is that these churches expect to draw people from a ten- to twenty-five-mile radius rather than from the neighborhood, and they project a distinctive identity. For many who come, the big bonus is that they are able to meet and make friends with people with similar interests, concerns, value systems, and religious orientation.

3. Focus on families that include preschool children. The centerpiece for this ministry often is the weekday nursery school that is supplemented by parenting classes, picnics, adult Bible study groups, and a dozen other programs.

Again a high fringe benefit is for parents to meet and make friends with people who share common concerns and values.

4. Focus on families with elementary school aged children. Again a big fringe benefit is the opportunity to meet people with similar interests, values, and concerns.

5. Focus on families with teenagers. Instead of concentrating on youth, build a package of ministries with both parents and youth. Music, parenting classes, mutual support groups, chess, Bible study, a strong recreation ministry, and big events often are central components of the total program.

6. Focus on mature adults. One approach is directed at that slice of the mature population who share most or all of these characteristics. They (a) enjoy a happy marriage and like to be in the company of their spouse; (b) have been looking forward to those carefree retirement years; (c) do not feel a compulsion to be needed and, therefore, find it easy to move from having been heavily involved in church as a volunteer to more of a spectator role; (d) enjoy the out-of-doors; (e) enjoy better-than-average health for their age group; (f) do not feel emotionally, psychologically, or economically dependent on their children; (g) enjoy their grandchildren—but usually at a distance; (h) prefer leisure activities that have clearly defined rules, boundaries, and terminations and offer immediate opportunities for the evaluation of one's performance (golf, service on single-purpose ad hoc task forces, bridge, travel); (i) prefer not to spend all day alone; (j) are comfortable making quick decisions that may have long-term implications; (k) benefit from an above-average income; (l) enjoy helping to pioneer the new, but show little interest in perpetuating the old; (m) display little interest in participating in intergenerational activities and are comfortable socializing

largely with people from their own generation; (n) find it relatively easy to switch denominational affiliation in the search for a new church home; and (o) accept and affirm the advantages of cremation far more readily than people from their generation who continue to live in the same community where they spent most of their adult life.

The most highly visible expression of these characteristics can be found in those retirement communities in the Sunbelt, organized around a golf course and a club house. A second is the crew of volunteers who annually spend two or three or more weeks constructing the meeting house for a new congregation or helping to rebuild a church that has been demolished by fire or the weather or building Habitat for Humanity houses for low-income families. A third is the work group that every year spends a few weeks in a mission station on another continent.

A substantially different approach, and the one most vigorously endorsed by the participants, is to challenge mature adults to be engaged in doing ministry on a continuing basis. This may include teaching in the Sunday school; participating in a surrogate Grandfathers' Club, which functions as an active support group for the weekday nursery school; organizing and nurturing the Mothers' Club for first-time mothers; replacing the paid custodian and maintaining the building and grounds; organizing and implementing a big capital funds campaign; sewing for missions; volunteering in a food pantry; or teaching four sessions of the 36-week new member orientation class.

This approach is designed to reach and include those mature adults who have a commitment to doing ministry; who are convinced they still have gifts, skills, and energy to offer to the church; who enjoy doing rather than being cared for; and to challenge those who enjoy being challenged.

7. Focus on worldwide missions. Plan to reach and challenge people who believe missions should be central to the life of any worshiping community. This alternative usually includes orga-

nizing mission work teams who spend two weeks to two or three years in a mission assignment, making missions the number-one priority for volunteers, allocating one-third to one-half of all dollar receipts to missions, and finding a pastor who sees missions as the number-one priority.

8. Build an issue-centered ministry. This means placing the prophetic voice of the church at the top of the agenda and attracting people who are convinced that the church should have a highly visible presence on issues such as gambling, abortion, peace, civil rights, and similar concerns. This often means a regional rather than a neighborhood role and drawing people from a ten- to twenty-mile radius.

9. If you follow a liturgical, or Eucharist-centered, approach to worship, seek to reach the refugees from nonliturgical churches who prefer Eucharist-centered worship. If you follow a less structured and nonliturgical format for worship, focus on the refugees from the liturgical churches. (This second migration is larger in numbers than the first.)

10. For many long-established small congregations, the easiest-to-implement alternative is to create an additional worship experience for the weekend, designed to reach and serve people who will not come to that "regular service" on Sunday morning.

One example is the new Saturday evening worship experience designed largely by and for young adults in the 17-25 age bracket.

For all practical purposes, this means (a) the pastor will be the part-time shepherd of that existing flock; (b) the pastor will become the part-time developer of what in effect is a new mission; (c) the pastor has to be enthusiastic about this dual role; (d) the members of the long-established congregation must be neutral to supportive of this venture, including use of their building as the meeting place for this "new mission"; (e) the pastor must be comfortable working with two very different groups of constituents; and (f) a response to the question "When will we merge these two congregations into one" should be postponed until the day, which may never come, when the members of that new congregation want to merge with the long-established congregation.

Perhaps the most common expression of this strategy consists of two components. First, guarantee the continuation of the "traditional" worship service at or near the traditional hour on Sunday morning. Second, create the new nontraditional worship experience at either an earlier or a later time for a new constituency.

11. Focus on the leisure-time population.[8] For many small town and rural congregations in Iowa, Florida, Missouri, North Carolina, New York, Pennsylvania, Arkansas, Oregon, Wisconsin, Minnesota, Texas, Arizona, and other states, a new option has emerged with the growth in the leisure-time constituencies. In Florida and Texas, it is the "snowbirds" who come to escape the winter cold. In Wisconsin and Michigan, the new constituency includes the urbanites who spend summer weekends at their cabin or cottage.

One of the products of affluence is the two-home family. For many, one residence is in Florida or Arizona or south Texas or Arkansas; the other is in the North. For others, one residence is near the place of work, and the second is near the place of recreation.

Three of the trends that have fed this pattern are (a) early retirement—nearly one-half of all American males are partially or fully retired by age sixty-two, (b) longer life expectancy and better health for mature adults, and (c) favorable federal tax laws.

This is not an easy alternative!

It is easier to sit, watch the congregation grow older and smaller, complain about how the tourists and seasonal residents are creating traffic jams and congestion in the restaurants, wonder why these folks do not want to come to our church and support our budget, or to explain that vacationers also are on vacation from church.

How does a small church reach seasonal visitors and tourists? Pick two or three of these alternatives as the initial points of contact: (a) Schedule the weekly Tuesday evening or Saturday evening dinner for the general public; (b) call on all seasonal residents; (c) schedule a big event every Thursday evening to which the general public is invited; (d) offer outstanding biblical preaching; (e) utilize direct-mail advertising; (f) offer outdoor worship experiences; (g) recruit newcomers and seasonal visitors for your drama group; (h) organize a choir from new retirees or seasonal residents; (i) offer Christian music concerts followed by a fellowship hour; (j) encourage your "repeat visitors" from last year to bring their friends; (k) invite known churchgoers from among the seasonal residents to serve on an ad hoc committee to design midweek or Saturday evening worship experiences for nonmembers; (l) schedule special Sundays for natives of another state—in Florida, schedule a special Sunday for seasonal residents from Pennsylvania, another for seasonal residents from New York—in Michigan, schedule one Sunday for seasonal residents from Ohio, another for seasonal residents from Indiana—in Texas or Oregon, schedule one Sunday for refugees from California. Schedule a picnic with a potluck meal for 12:30 Sunday, after church for natives of that particular state.

Use your imagination and call on your most creative members to help create new entry points.

12. Become a multicultural congregation. This also is one of the more difficult-to-implement alternatives on this list. If it were easy, we would have far more multicultural congregations than now exist.

Five different strategies begin to illustrate the range of possibilities.

(a) The easiest is for the congregation with a pastor married to a spouse from another race or cultural heritage to take the lead in projecting an identity that "This is the Protestant church for couples who come from an international or intercultural or interracial marriage."

(b) Appeal to parents, many of whom reside in culturally and racially homogeneous neighborhoods, to perceive that this is the church where their children can enjoy and grow in a multicultural environment. This, again, usually means a regional role.

(c) Build a bivocational pastoral staff of three ministers from three different cultural or racial or language or ethnic heritages. That bivocational team can model new relationships for both adults and children.

(d) If your location makes this a viable alternative, become the multicultural church for students, administrators, and faculty from that nearby university.

(e) If the church is located in a multicultural residential area, concentrate on building relationships between members and nearby residents by picnics, social events, visitation, athletic teams (make sure each team is a multicultural squad!), eating together, and mutual support groups.

While exceptions do exist, it usually is much easier for a congregation on the conservative half of the theological spectrum to become a multicultural parish than it is for the church located near the liberal end of that spectrum.

13. Use television to reach and invite strangers. Television is now the single most effective tool for inviting strangers to come to church. Three cautions should be mentioned. First, as in all forms of advertising, repetition is important. Therefore, do not be impatient. Persist!

Second, the quality of the message must be competitive with network quality. Find volunteers with genuine expertise to produce your videotapes or hire professionals.

Third, television is not effective in the advertising of institutions. It works best with attractive personalities. Therefore, the pastor must be both able and willing to become the symbol for your church to that television audience.

14. Carve out a distinctive niche.[9] If you are one of three or more congregations affiliated with the same denomination in that general community, identify and fill a clearly defined niche. This can be based on music, place on the theological spectrum, constituency, schedule, specialized programming, or some other characteristic. This is the nonliturgical Lutheran parish. This is the evangelical United Methodist congregation. This is the Disciples of Christ congregation with the growing youth ministry. This is the church with the exceptionally attractive forty-minute teaching sermon every Sunday morning.

15. The world is filled with hurting people who feel that no one understands them. Identify and build a new constituency through the creation of several mutual support or Twelve-Step or recovery groups. One may be for younger adults dealing with the impact of their parents' divorce when they were twelve. A second for recovering alcoholics. A third for parents who have experienced the death of a child. A fourth for the recently widowed. A fifth for formerly married adults embarking on a new marriage. Add one or two new groups every year. This alternative has been chosen and effectively implemented by hundreds of small churches in large central cities.

The key to this alternative is highly competent volunteer leadership.

16. Focus on the unchurched. For the vast majority of small churches, this is the most difficult of all alternatives in this chapter. The explanation of that statement is the theme of the first chapter. Most small congregations are predominantly second-commandment churches. Most unchurched individuals who do become regular churchgoers are attracted to first-commandment parishes that focus on meeting the religious needs of people.

That, however, does not close out this option for small churches! The second-commandment congregation that lives out the command to love one's neighbor by how the people live their lives can win converts to Jesus Christ. They do it less by words and more by deeds. The agnostics, atheists, and the believers who are disillusioned with the institutional expression of God's church can be won by the second-commandment parishes. Try it. It can be done.

Leaders Do Lead!

Seeking to identify tomorrow's potential constituency, their needs, and how your congregation can respond to those needs may be the best approach to planning for tomorrow in most small Protestant congregations in North America. Far more popular, far more widely used, and far easier for most congregational leaders is a second approach. This can be summarized in this wish, "If we can find the right pastor who is a skilled leader, our troubles will be behind us."

One reason why that wish is articulated so often is that sometimes it works. Scores of what today are vital, strong, ministry-driven, attractive, and exciting congregations once were small and shrinking churches that appeared to have a severely limited future. For some reason, God brought that collection of worshipers together with an exceptionally gifted leader. Within a few years, the results of that match far exceeded anyone's most optimistic dreams.

Gifted, skilled, visionary, and transformational pastoral leadership can turn and has turned a dying congregation into the strongest church in that community. Never underestimate the potential of exceptionally high-quality pastoral leadership! There are, however, two cautions that need to be added to that observation.

First, the best environment for that leadership to maximize the potential is in planting a new congregation. The task of transforming the small and long-established parish that has spent the past several years watching the members grow older in age and fewer in number is a huge challenge for even the most gifted leaders.

Second, the demand for energetic and creative pastors, who also are deeply committed Christians, attractive personalities, future-oriented, and highly skilled transformational leaders and productive workers far exceeds the supply. The ratio may be close to one hundred to one.

A more modest version of this approach is to recognize the merits of identifying the strengths, assets, gifts, experience, skills, and personality of the present pastor. When that is the appropriate beginning point, ten different and attractive courses of action can be identified. The number-one criterion in choosing from among these possibilities is this: Which one comes closest to matching the competence, gifts, and preferences of this minister?

The number-two criterion is: Which alternative matches the local congregational culture, the community setting, the assets this collection of people bring to the planning process, the gifts of the volunteer leaders, and the unmet needs of people?

What Are the Choices?

These ten alternatives are not presented in any particular order of importance, but the second and third do place the greatest responsibilities on the pastor as a transformational leader.

1. Raise the level of quality. This is the least likely to be disruptive, the most likely to win support, and also the most likely to produce the greatest immediate impact.

This may mean raising the quality of the preaching or enhancing the quality of the teaching ministry or improving the quality of the meeting place or elevating the quality of worship or expanding and improving the quality of the caring for one another or enriching the ministry of music.

This can mean accepting and openly affirming that primary role as a second-commandment church. This world needs more high-quality second-commandment churches! The

Stephen Ministries (8016 Dale Avenue, St. Louis, MO 63117-1449) offer excellent training for leaders who train members to become competent, compassionate, and effective caregivers. Enroll three or four or five leaders in this program and ask them to train one-half of the members to serve as caregivers. That can be the most effective means of raising the level of quality in the small second-commandment church. The downside of this alternative is that small congregations with a high-quality caring ministry rarely remain small. They grow up out of that size bracket.

2. Become a high-quality first-commandment church. This usually requires a two-step process of first greatly expanding and enriching the group life of the small church. The focal point for carrying out the second of Jesus' two great commandments is gradually and largely transferred from the congregation as a whole to classes, choirs, circles, cells, groups, organizations, and other subgroups within the congregation. This first step can be supplemented and reinforced by the training of lay volunteers to become Stephen Ministers in that congregation. (See the preceding paragraph for address.)

The old self-image of a congregation of sixty or one hundred or two hundred individuals is replaced by a new self-image as a congregation of classes, choirs, circles, cells, and other subgroups. These are the focal points for caring and for strengthening the horizontal relationships. The top priority in the congregation as a whole is that first commandment of Jesus.

Concurrent with the expansion and enrichment of the group life comes that second step. This is to enlarge and enhance the capability of that congregation to respond in meaningful ways to the religious needs of people. This often begins with the creation of new adult Bible study groups, the addition of other learning opportunities, the introduction of drama into worship, the creation of one or two new mutual support groups every year, strengthening the ministry of music, raising the quality and relevance of the preaching, an expansion of the adult Sunday school, and the addition of a twelve- to forty-five-week inquirer's class for searchers, seekers, pilgrims, self-identified agnostics, and others who see themselves as on a faith journey.

Perhaps the most subtle, but extremely important, component of the process in this strategy is to change the definition of church membership. Instead of identifying the act of uniting with this congregation as a destination, it is perceived as a doorway. Newcomers pass through that doorway to new learning opportunities, spiritual growth experiences, discipling classes, and challenges to be engaged in doing ministry.

For many small second-commandment congregations, another change also is part of this alternative course of action. This is to move from projecting modest to low expectations of people in terms of Christian commitment (Christian commitment is not the same as institutional loyalty!) to high expectations. These high-expectation congregations challenge people to become all that God expects of them.

This shift to becoming *predominantly* a first-commandment church and secondarily a collection of second-commandment subgroups is the most effective means of reaching, attracting, serving, and assimilating a new generation into what once was *predominantly* a second-commandment church.

It is not easy! This shift requires radical change. It requires a pastor who combines transformational leadership skills with a compelling vision of a new tomorrow, a deep commitment to the goal of making this a congregation that projects high expectations of people, a high level of skill in interpersonal relationships, far above average competence as a preacher and teacher, and unusually productive work habits.

3. Relocate to a new site and become a regional church. This may be the most difficult to implement of any of the alternatives in this chapter. Why?

Implementation of this alternative requires many changes, including (1) a shift from a self-identified small church to a regional identity; (2) replacing a tradition-driven approach to planning and decision making with a powerful future orientation and outreach-driven approach; (3) placing the identification and serving of a new constituency ahead of taking care of today's members on the new list of priorities; (4) the transformation from *predominantly* a second-commandment congregation to becoming *predominantly* a first-commandment church; (5) raising the level of quality in all facets of ministry; (6) mobilizing large amounts of money to finance the relocation effort; (7) an acceptance of the fact that most relocation efforts are rejected the first time or two they are proposed and developing the persistence to continue pushing that compelling vision;[10] (8) a high level of skill at initiating change from within an organization; (9) an ability to accept the fact that one price tag on radical change often is the departure of several long-time pillars; (10) an acceptance of the claim that the automobile is here to stay and that the geographically defined parish is a concept of the pre-automobile era; (11) a willingness to think in terms of incremental change—functioning for several years as a two-site congregation often is a part of this long-term strategy; and (12) a long pastorate.

That is a heavy load and explains why seven other less radical changes belong on this list.

4. Shift from a focus on the first person of the Trinity to the second. Many small second-commandment congregations place the greatest emphasis on God the Creator. This can be seen in the preaching, in the choice of hymns, in public prayers, and in priorities in mission and outreach. If the goal is to reach the generations born after 1955, place a greater emphasis on Jesus the Savior.

5. Increase the emphasis on intercessory prayer. The creation of prayer chains, the organization of new Bible study and prayer groups, and the scheduling of occasional prayer retreats can be a means of meeting the religious needs of many people in a manner that is both compatible with and supportive of that

second-commandment congregational culture and with reaching new generations of churchgoers.

It should be obvious, of course, that both of these last two alternatives require a pastor, or a bivocational pastoral team, who is ideologically, theologically, and personally supportive of that particular alternative.

6. Switch from a topical or pastoral counseling approach to preaching, both of which are compatible with the second-commandment congregational culture, to expository sermons. Nurture those who come to have their faith strengthened.

A greater emphasis on preaching as teaching can be a modest step toward a "both-and" balance in comparing the second-commandment congregation with the first-commandment focus.

7. Raise expectations. This requires a long pastorate with a minister who is committed to the concept that one means of enriching the spiritual journey of people is to raise expectations. This is a single-step alternative and is far less demanding and disruptive than alternatives 2 and 3, described earlier.

The central component of this strategy is to shift from projecting high expectations of people in terms of what they give to the church (time and money) to concentrate on what people can receive through prayer, study, challenges, learning, and outreach.

8. Accelerate the pace of worship. What do many young people say when asked why they rarely share in the corporate worship of God in the second-commandment congregation? The most common response is "It's dull and boring."

Worship in the second-commandment church naturally resembles the pace of a leisurely dinner or an hour-long visit. The pace is slow and includes many moments of silence.

Back in the 1950s, baseball was a highly popular game among young people. For most of the players on the team, one-half of the time is spent standing around watching two players throw the ball back and forth. Occasionally one or two other players will be actively involved in catching or throwing the ball. A full half inning may go by in which one-third to two-thirds of the team in the field never touch the ball while it is in play. During the other half of the inning most of the players sit while one attempts to hit the ball. Occasionally one or two or three others will be running the bases. In most innings, however, one-half of the players never touch the bat or a base. Baseball is largely a spectator sport for the players.

Today many young people prefer to play soccer or basketball rather than baseball. Soccer, like basketball, is a fast-paced and high-energy game in which everyone on the team is in motion and frequent opportunities come along to touch the ball. Basketball, like soccer, is a participatory game for the players. Many young people prefer it to baseball.

The parallel is that an increasing proportion of the adult population prefers a fast-paced worship experience with a high level of active participation by the congregation to the slower paced spectator type of worship service that was so common back in the 1950s.

This change also requires the leadership of a pastor who is comfortable with a fast-paced, participatory, and celebrative approach to worship. It also requires an openness to recent generations of contemporary Christian music.

9. Offer hope. An ancient bit of advice to preachers declares that every sermon should include a word of comfort and end on a note of hope.

In many of today's small congregations, pessimism about the future dominates the agenda. This is especially common in those second-commandment congregations in which the "young people" are in their fifties.

One beginning point to the future can be to point out that the glass is not simply half empty, but it also is half full. One purpose of this chapter is to point out that nearly every small church on the North American continent is faced, not with only two or three alternatives, but with at least eight to ten. The choices are greater than many people believe.

10. Become part of a larger cooperative parish.[11] While this alternative is less popular than it was in the 1960s, a tenth alternative is to join with two to twenty other small churches to create a cooperative arrangement that can build on the strengths of the participating congregations.

If the primary motivation in creating this cooperative arrangement is to (a) guarantee each congregation the part-time services of a fully credentialed minister or (b) save money, the results may not meet expectations.

If, however, the primary motivation is expanded outreach, responding to the religious needs of people, involving the laity in doing ministry, and offering a stronger Christian witness in the larger community, the cooperative parish can be an attractive alternative.

This, too, requires the active and supportive leadership of the pastor or of that bivocational pastoral team.

Why Not Begin with Program?

A third set of beginning points for examining alternatives open to the leaders of the small church is to look at the total program and how it can be strengthened. One reason for not offering this first is that it tends to encourage and reinforce a producer's perspective. Instead of beginning with the religious and personal needs of tomorrow's constituency, this focus on program may tempt people to conclude, "Let's do yesterday over again, only better." A second reason for not beginning with program is the local priorities will depend in part on the gifts, skills, experiences, preferences, energy, vision, and available time of the pastor and volunteer leaders.

A good reason for using program as the beginning point is that most small congregations include several creative and deeply committed individuals who are both willing and able to help pioneer new ministries and programs. Frequently, however, the first step requires an answer to that question, "What should we do?" Here are seven responses to that question.

1. Schedule four to ten major events and festivals annually. Create new entry points by inviting nonmembers to attend these events. Each one is a separate and free-standing event that stands by itself. Each one is based on the assumption that it is easier to return to a new place the second time than it is to go there the first time. Thus first-time visitors who attend one of these events will find it easier to return later.

(a) Plan a "birthday party for Jesus" at about 4:30 P.M. on December 24. Invite all the children in your larger community who were born during the past three years. Many will not comprehend the full theological significance of the virgin birth, but most know what a birthday party is. Send the invitation to the child, not to the parents. Parents are welcome, but your primary guests are the young children.

(b) Schedule a Constitution Day celebration every July and celebrate the freedom of religion guaranteed in the First Amendment to the Constitution. Invite teachers, community leaders, people engaged in law enforcement, and government officials to be your guests.

(c) Invite every adult who lives alone to come and eat Thanksgiving dinner at your church. Make this a joyful annual festival. Empty-nest couples could serve as the hosts.

(d) Instead of ending vacation Bible school on Friday, schedule the last gathering for Sunday morning. Celebrate the learnings and accomplishments of the past week.

(e) Organize a community-wide garage sale every August with the proceeds going to help alleviate world hunger.

(f) Schedule on the second or third Sunday of June every year a time when couples can come and renew their marriage vows. Plan a special celebration for those celebrating their tenth, twenty-fifth, and fiftieth anniversaries. Close with refreshments, fellowship, and the presentation of awards or pins.

(g) Schedule a Sunday in late August or early September to welcome all newcomers to the community who have moved here during the past twelve months.

(h) Design your service for Labor Day Sunday as a time to honor the labors of all educators in your community. Send a personal invitation to every educator in your community to come and worship with you and to be recognized for their labors.

(i) Create a community drama group composed of both members and nonmembers that will produce one religious play annually. Invite the general public to attend.

(j) Schedule a Tuesday evening forum for voters in the community to come and hear a debate among the candidates for public office.

These are offered as examples of events that can be scheduled to help outsiders become better acquainted with your congregation.

2. Change the music. Examine the possibility of using some of the Christian music created since 1970.

3. Become a seven-day-a-week church. Instead of scheduling most religious activities for Sunday, add one new weekday class or program to the schedule annually. Within a decade, this can transform your congregation into a seven-day-a-week church with two or three events scheduled for every day of the week. Each one of these can become an entry point for future new members.

4. Accept the role as the church in your community that places a high priority on inculcating into the next generations traditional Christian moral values and standards of ethical behavior. The best beginning point may be the weekday nursery school for pre-kindergarten children. The second best may be a children's choir or a youth group for grades 5-8. The third best could be a chess club for third and fourth graders. Among other advantages, chess teaches that present actions have future consequences.

5. If that works, add kindergarten to the weekday schedule. A year later, add a first-grade class. The following year, add a second-grade class. This could be combined with an effort that began earlier to reach and serve parents who are home schoolers and who seek a place for structured socialization experiences for their children three or four or five afternoons every week.

6. Hustle what you have! An old saying in show business is "Hustle what you have!" It means promote what you do best. The translation for the small church is to identify what that congregation excels in and seek to reinforce, strengthen, expand, and give greater visibility to that particular ministry, program, choir, class, or experience. What do you do best? Brag about it. Improve it! Give it greater visibility!

7. Become a grant-giving church. The generations of residents of the United States born before 1935 have accumulated well over $5 trillion in wealth. Many of these are active churchgoers. A disproportionately large number are in small second-commandment churches affiliated with one of the "mainline" Protestant denominations. Encourage your members to remember the church in their will.

While many readers will reject this out of hand, it is a viable alternative for 5 to 10 percent of all small second-commandment congregations. Each one could create an endowment fund, which in twenty years will exceed $2 million. The income from investments can be used to finance a variety of outreach ministries.

The big difference between this short list of seven alternatives under program and the sixteen possibilities described earlier is this list begins with this question: What are the potentialities within this congregation for expanding the program to reach a larger number of people? That earlier and longer list begins with a different question: What are the religious and personal needs of people that we can address?

Institutional Relationships

A fourth set of alternatives for the small church begins with the fact that every congregation is an institution. In most states, each congregation is a legally incorporated, nonprofit corporation.

1. The most exciting possibility from this perspective is for this small congregation to accept the initiating leadership role for creating a network of new nonprofit 501(c)3 corporations. One could focus on the rehabilitation of housing for low-income families. A second could concentrate on economic development in that community. A third could feed the hungry. A fourth could shelter the homeless. A fifth could offer drug rehabilitation. A sixth could be a halfway house for people released from prison. A seventh could operate a private Christian school. An eighth might provide job training. The worshiping community would be the hub in this network of separate nonprofit institutions.[12]

2. For perhaps 30 to 40 percent of all second-commandment congregations, one potential role for tomorrow would be a close relationship with another institution. This congregation could relate to the residents of the nearby nursing home. That one could relate to the patients and their families plus the staff of the hospital down the street. Another could be the church that relates to the regional or national headquarters of the denomination that is housed in a nearby office structure. Occasionally the regional judicatory could be housed in that small congregation's building.

The most promising is to build a three-way partnership with the principal and teachers in a nearby elementary school plus the parents of the children enrolled in that school. The point of commonality is the welfare of those children. Your congregation could offer an after-school program and/or parenting classes and/or a prekindergarten nursery school and/or other services. Currently the interest in this three-way partnership appears to be greatest among elementary school principals and lowest among short-tenured pastors.

This partnership could be incorporated as a separate 501(c)3 nonprofit corporation and be the recipient of grants from individuals, foundations, governmental bodies, and corporations.

3. Do not close! Instead of closing or dissolving, the course of action taken by more than sixty Protestant congregations in the average week, a different alternative choice is to be "adopted" as a "wounded bird" by a large congregation with discretionary resources.[13] The responsibility for the administration of that wounded bird is given to the missionary church. The volunteer leaders from that missionary church help the wounded bird redefine a new goal and assist in mobilizing the resources necessary to fulfill that new role. When the wounded bird is healed, it flies off on its own in a new direction with renewed vigor.

This third alternative replaces the denominational headquarters with a missionary church as the healing center for wounded birds. In some denominations, the polity may rule out this possibility.

Alternatives in Staffing

While it is a means-to-an-end issue and can become subversive of religious goals, many people prefer to start with a fifth set of alternatives. This is the question of staffing the small church with pastoral leadership.

In recent years, the costs to a congregation for the compensation package of a fully credentialed, full-time resident pastor have been rising at a faster pace than the increase in congregational income. Four major alternatives stand out as beginning points if this is to be the focal point for planning for the twenty-first century.

1. The bivocational pastor. The fastest growing among these four alternatives is the bivocational pastor. This is the less than full-time pastor, often nonresident, who serves one small congregation. A reasonable guess is that somewhere between 75,000 and 100,000 congregations are utilizing this alternative in the United States in the closing years of the twentieth century.[14]

In one community, an elementary school principal is the weekend pastor of a small church. In another, an attorney who took early retirement at age fifty-eight is the part-time pastor of a congregation meeting in a building thirty miles from that lawyer's residence. In another, a seminary graduate and the father of three young children is the primary houseparent in his family and pastors a small church while his wife serves as a physician on the staff of a medical clinic.

The combinations are countless, but each congregation enjoys all of the time of its pastor all Sunday morning plus several hours during the rest of the week. One major fringe benefit is that it strengthens the responsibilities of the laity in each congregation.

This is a most attractive alternative for congregations averaging fewer than 40 to 60 at worship.

2. The bivocational team. Less common, but also growing very rapidly, is the emergence of the three- to five-member lay team. Together they serve as the pastoral team of a congregation averaging 60 to 120 at worship.

One member of this lay team is the preacher. Another is the minister of music. A third is responsible for the teaching ministry. A fourth is a trained Stephen Minister who trains volunteers for the ministry of pastoral care. The fifth may be the liturgist or the administrator or the youth director or the evangelist, depending on the mix of gifts among the other members of that team and the volunteers in that congregation. One or more persons on this bivocational team may come out of the membership of that church.

The cost to the congregation for the expenses and compensation of the bivocational team usually is one-tenth to one-half of the compensation of a fully credentialed full-time pastor.

One of the big fringe benefits is that the continuity is in the team, not in one individual. Thus only minimal disruption results when one member departs for the team continues. The team socializes the replacement in "how we do things here." The team provides an immediate and continuing support system for that new member of the team.

The downside of this alternative is that the congregation may increase in numbers to the point that the workload for the team exceeds their discretionary time and energy, but no one wants to replace the team with a full-time pastor.

3. The circuit or yoked field. While it is decreasing in popularity, the concept of one full-time pastor concurrently serving two or three or four or five congregations still has many advocates.

Among the reasons for the declining popularity of this alternative are these five: (a) A serious mismatch can have a highly disruptive impact on two or more congregations, not simply on one. (b) The schedule means that the pastor cannot be present for all of Sunday morning in any one church, and that can undermine the teaching ministry. (c) It has turned out to be the next-to-last step in the process of closing literally thousands of small Protestant congregations. (d) Too often the participating congregations are selected on the basis of geographical proximity, rather than similarities in culture, theological stance, or needs. (e) The resulting stress on the pastor often results in short pastorates.

4. Other short-term solutions. The fourth alternative is to assume that small churches will benefit from short pastorates and pursue that arrangement. One is the student pastorate of two to four years. Another is the retired minister who comes for a postretirement pastorate of three to five years. A third is the

teacher at the nearby college or seminary or the institutional chaplain who "fills in" for a couple of years.

If the top priority is to provide postseminary graduation employment for pastors, the circuit has a role. If short-term pastorates are deemed acceptable, the brief tenure of the student pastor or the postretirement minister has a place. If, however, the goal is to strengthen the life and ministry of the small church, the bivocational pastor and the bivocational team appear to be the most attractive alternatives.

Is Survival the Issue?

Finally, another set of four alternatives merits mention if everyone agrees that institutional survival is the number-one issue facing that small church. This list is both last and brief because these should be considered only after all other possibilities have been studied and rejected.

1. Subsidies for survival. The most widely followed is the use of financial subsidies to pay the bills and keep the doors open. In a few, but growing number of small congregations, the financial subsidies come from (a) those occasional bequests left by generous members, (b) income from an endowment fund, or (c) the sale of assets, such as land or stocks or bonds.

In many more, the subsidy comes from denominational headquarters. The Episcopal Church once was the leader in subsidizing small missions for decades, but in recent years The United Methodist Church has moved to the forefront. The subsidies may be direct, such as cash grants or supplementing the pastor's salary. They may be indirect, such as providing free services to the congregations or in paying the cost of fringe benefits (health insurance, pension, continuing education, etc.) for the pastor.

In several Protestant traditions, survival subsidies no longer are granted because of the natural tendency to (a) create dependency, (b) stifle member giving, and (c) nurture an adversarial relationship between the subsidized congregation and the regional judicatory providing that financial subsidy. They have been replaced by short-term matching grants, requiring matching contributions from the members, for developing new ministries, and for expanding congregational outreach.

2. Merge with another congregation. A second alternative for survival is to merge with another congregation. A review of the results of scores of mergers involving small congregations suggests that the most common result five or ten years later is that the merged congregation is no larger than the bigger of the two that decided to unite.[15]

The best results tend to come from a merger of three congregations, no one of which is larger than the combined size of the other two, with a clearly defined and widely supported goal of creating a new congregation that will meet in a new building at a new location under a new name with a new role and new pastoral leadership.

3. While far less common today than it was in the 1925–40 era, the concept of the federated church still has its supporters. This approach calls for two or three congregations from different religious traditions to come together and to function as one congregation with one governing board, one budget, and one staff, but two or three membership rosters. This arrangement enables everyone who wishes to retain membership in his or her own denominational family. New members choose the denominational label they want to carry.

In recent years, many denominational leaders have encouraged federated congregations to choose one denomination, strengthen its ties to that one tradition, and terminate the relationships to other denominations. This has been more common in white Midwestern congregations than elsewhere.

4. Close or disband. Finally, it must be recognized that several hundred Protestant congregations close every year. Dissolution, like death, should be seen as the last alternative.

If agreement is reached that disbanding is the best available course of action, that decision should include the scheduling of a final worship service that celebrates and gives thanks to God for this ministry over the years. End with a celebration, not a whimper.

What Are the Implications?

Once upon a time, the conventional wisdom advised the newly arrived pastor to spend a year or so building relationships with the pillars of that congregation, to discover the distinctive culture of that congregation, to "learn the lay of the land," and to earn acceptance.

Likewise, for many decades the staff of the regional judicatory of that denomination placed a high priority on ministerial placement and on the care of pastors.

If, and this is a big if, the primary need is to help that small church carve out a new role for itself for the third millennium, a new responsibility has moved to the top of the agenda for that recently arrived pastor or that staff person from the regional judicatory. The new challenge is to help the leaders of the small church identify their future constituency. That means shifting from a producer to a consumer orientation.

Once upon a time, many small churches enjoyed an automatic constituency. For one group of congregations, this was the common identity of the members in terms of nationality, language, customs, and inherited religious affiliation. The Lutheran immigrants from Sweden attended a Swedish Lutheran church.

For others, it was race or geographical proximity to the meeting place or inherited denominational loyalties or social class or kinship ties or a common enemy or a forty-year pastorate or occupation. The open country church in the farming community was the most highly visible of congregations organized around a common occupation.

Today, few congregations have an automatic constituency. Thanks to the automobile, a greater sense of individual autonomy, affluence, the erosion of inherited institutional loyalties, the increased geographical separation of the place of residence from the place of work, the rise in the level of competition among the churches, the demand for choices in this consumer-driven society, the rise in ecumenism which legitimatizes the ministries of churches from other traditions, and interdenominational and interfaith marriages, that automatic constituency no longer exists for most churches.

What are the implications? For many newly arrived pastors, this often means making the identification of a new constituency an early and high priority. For the staff of the regional judicatory, it often means that strategy development moves ahead of ministerial placement as the most urgent need. It often means accepting the role of the outside third-party interventionist in helping congregations plan for a new tomorrow. Ideally, that will be accomplished before the process of ministerial placement begins.

In more specific terms, it means that the staff of that regional judicatory should be (1) eager to accept the role as an interventionist; (2) prepared to suggest the planning model that is appropriate for each particular combination of circumstances; (3) able to help the leaders of that small congregation build a long list of alternative possibilities; (4) willing to challenge local leaders to consider alternatives they believe are beyond their capabilities; (5) ready to accept the role as cheerleader when that is needed; (6) prepared to help each congregation define the criteria for reducing that list of alternatives to two or three; (7) reluctant to encourage dissolutions or mergers; (8) able to encourage the scheduling of three or more meetings in order to give congregational leaders time (a) for their second thoughts and (b) to talk themselves into alternatives that may have been rejected prematurely; (9) prepared to display an admirable degree of patience; (10) reluctant to encourage requests for financial subsidies; (11)

committed to keeping the focus on purpose, outreach, and ministry, and placing means-to-an-end issues (staffing, money, real estate, institutional goals) lower on the agenda; and (12) able to affirm less-than-perfect compromises.

From the perspective of that newly arrived pastor, the two big overlapping challenges often are (1) balancing a concern with taking care of the members with cultivating tomorrow's new constituency and (2) keeping institutional maintenance goals no higher than second place on the local agenda below the need to be in touch with the changing religious needs of that passing parade of people called a worshiping community.

The easy alternative is to watch passively as congregations grow older and smaller.

6.

WHAT HAVE WE LEARNED?

I
t seems to me that with all the studies of small churches that have been completed over the past forty years, we must have learned something that could be helpful," observed a long-tenured leader in a congregation that has been averaging between sixty and seventy at worship for the past several decades. "What do we have to show for all that research? What have we learned?"

That is a fair question. We have learned a lot. A few of these learnings can be summarized here.

Perhaps the most significant learning, but one that is yet to be fully accepted, is that no one congregation can meet the religious needs of all the residents of a community or neighborhood. This learning runs contrary to the dreams of the social reformers and experts who, from 1880 to 1980, opposed the overchurching of both rural and urban communities. Their goal was no more than one church per 1,000 residents. This contrasted with the ratio of one church for every 403 residents reported in the 1906 Census of Religious Bodies, conducted by the United States Bureau of the Census. It also contrasts with the ratio of one church for every

700 residents in the United States in 1994 and one church per 400 residents of rural areas.

This learning also runs counter to the wishes of many church leaders today who believe that any one congregation can and should "be all things to all people." Every congregation should be able to respond effectively to the religious needs of every person who lives within a mile of that church's meeting place.

That is a fair expectation to place on the Universal Church, but it is an unrealistic expectation to place on any one congregation. It is an especially unreasonable expectation to place on a small congregation with limited resources that is equipped to proclaim the gospel in only one or two or three languages. This helps to explain why the dreams of the social reformers of the first half of the twentieth century have not been fulfilled. (See chapter 3.)

A second learning, and one that also has encountered considerable opposition, is that most English language congregations on the North American continent are in competition with at least two or three other congregations for the next generation of new members. The automobile has become the great equalizer, expanding the range of options available to most churchgoers.

Overlapping that is a third learning. For most people choosing a new church home, geographical convenience has dropped below quality, relevance, kinship ties, and denominational label as a factor in making that decision.

A fourth learning, and the primary reason for writing this book, consists of two opposing themes. On the one hand, stability, not numerical growth, is a natural characteristic of most small Protestant congregations. To grow in numbers usually requires radical change. That is difficult in any institution organized around (a) nurturing one-to-one relationships, (b) continuity with the past, and (c) a producer orientation.

On the other hand, hundreds of small churches have demonstrated that change is possible. The small church can reach large numbers of people. It can change. The key learning here is that this usually requires (a) concentrating on the religious needs of strangers and/or (b) skilled pastoral leadership. The first twenty-six alternative courses of action described in chapter 5 suggest ways for the small church to grow by following one of those alternatives.

While it is seldom mentioned in contemporary writings about the small church, a fifth learning is that words such as *routine, mundane, ordinary, commonplace,* and *humdrum* come closer than terms like *exciting, adventurous, romantic, transcendent,* or *transformational* in describing everyday life in the typical small church.[1]

A sixth learning, which was documented in chapter 2, is that the small congregation averaging fewer than a hundred people at worship is the normative institutional expression of North American Protestantism.

A seventh learning is that the pattern described in the preceding paragraph is widely identified as a "problem" by denominational leaders and many pastors, but is far less likely to be identified as a problem by the lifelong members of that small church.

An eighth learning is that the best of our small congregations are not simply miniature versions of larger churches. They are different orders of God's creation. That is the central theme of the first two chapters of this book. The central cohesive and unifying threads in the small church consist of local traditions, the people, and their relationships with one another. By contrast, the large church is organized around the staff, the program, the group life, worship, music, the teaching ministries, change, goals, identity, and the personality of the senior pastor.

Perhaps the most difficult lesson to communicate to leaders in the typical small congregation is that the future offers them more choices than they believe are out there. That is one of the central themes of the preceding chapter. God is giving them the opportunity to shape the future of that congregation!

Finally, and perhaps most important, we have learned that not every small church needs a full-time, fully credentialed, ordained minister to be effective. Bivocational pastors and bivocational ministerial teams have demonstrated that the laity can be entrusted with those leadership responsibilities. That may be the most significant learning for those concerned with the future of the small church in a society dominated by big institutions.

NOTES

Introduction

1. This introductory paragraph highlighting the symbolic importance of the fall of the Berlin Wall and the Israeli-Palestinian Accords represents the perspective of a mature adult. People born in 1974 and 1975 look at the world from a different perspective. A group of college and university freshmen in the 1992–93 academic year were asked what social and political events had happened during their formative years to shape their worldview. The most common response was the explosion of the *Challenger* space shuttle in January 1986. The second most widely mentioned event was the end of the Cold War, followed by the Persian Gulf War, the spread of AIDS, and the beating of Rodney King by Los Angeles police officers. See Arthur Levine, "The Making of a Generation," *Change* (September/October 1993): 8-15.

2. See Stephen L. Carter, *The Culture of Disbelief* (New York: Basic Books, 1993).

3. See Lyle E. Schaller, *21 Bridges to the 21st Century* (Nashville: Abingdon Press, 1994), chapter 15.

4. Several of these points were discussed in an earlier book. Lyle E. Schaller, *The Small Church Is Different!* (Nashville: Abingdon Press, 1982), pp. 17-55.

5. This point is discussed in greater detail in Lyle E. Schaller, *Strategies for Change* (Nashville: Abingdon Press, 1993), pp. 10-11, 15-30, 113-19.

6. This distinction is described in greater detail in Lyle E. Schaller, *The Seven-Day-A-Week Church* (Nashville: Abingdon Press, 1992).

1. The Second Great Commandment

1. Ray Oldenburg, *The Great Good Place* (New York: Paragon House, 1991).

2. For a provocative essay on how one large church combines the second commandment approach to congregational life with a strong teaching ministry, see Jackson W. Carroll, "Horizontal Religion," *The Christian Century* (October 13, 1993): 964-66.

3. For a long discussion on this subject, see Lyle E. Schaller, *Assimilating New Members* (Nashville: Abingdon Press, 1978).

4. Off-campus ministries is the theme of chapters 6 and 8 of Lyle E. Schaller, *Innovations in Ministry* (Nashville: Abingdon Press, 1994).

5. Carl Dudley, *Making the Small Church Effective* (Nashville: Abingdon Press, 1979).

6. The four yearnings people bring to church are described and discussed by Robert Randall, *What People Expect from Church* (Nashville: Abingdon Press, 1992).

7. See Ruth Wallace, *They Call Her Pastor* (Albany: State University of New York, 1992). For one recent evaluation of efforts to have one priest serve several Catholic congregations, see Joan C. McKeown, *Sharing More Than a Pastor* (Grantsburg, Wis.: Arc Research Co., 1993).

2. Why Are Small Churches Small?

1. In 1990, 32 of the 3,140 counties in the United States reported that their population was between 460 and 1,222. These counties included 28,000 residents and 144 Christian congregations, or an average of one church per 195 residents. Thus 1 percent of all U.S. counties included 0.011 percent of the nation's population and 0.024 percent of the nation's churches. It is unwise to generalize from a small proportion of the universe, but these figures illustrate the pattern that the lower the population, the more churches per 1,000 residents.

2. See Edward W. Hassinger et al., *The Rural Church: Learning from Three Decades of Experience* (Nashville: Abingdon Press, 1988).

3. Compete or Cooperate?

1. "Denominational Switching Is Common in U.S.," *PRRC Emerging Trends* (May 1992).
2. Eric F. Goldman, *Rendezvous with Destiny* (New York: Alfred A. Knoff, 1953).
3. One of the earliest of these reformers was the Congregational minister Washington Gladden. In a series of essays in *The Century Magazine* in 1882–83, Gladden advocated that denominations control the number of churches in order to reduce competition in a particular community. Gladden's basic thesis was that a few large churches would better serve the residents than many small congregations. He also contended that existing congregations should be favored over proposed new missions. By 1890, several denominational leaders had come together to create a comity agreement for New England. In today's world, comity would be seen as an effort to restrain trade by limiting the number of new missions that could enter the ecclesiastical marketplace.
4. For this entire account, I am greatly indebted to James H. Madison, "Reformers and the Rural Church, 1900-1950" in *The Journal of American History* 73 (1986): 645-68.
5. An appraisal of the origins of comity and its limitations can be found in Lyle E. Schaller, *Planning for Protestantism in Urban America* (Nashville: Abingdon Press, 1965), pp. 96-120.
6. A brief account of how other vacuums have been filled by new churches in recent years is Lyle E. Schaller, *Innovations in Ministry* (Nashville: Abingdon Press, 1994), chapter 2.
7. An iconoclastic analysis of interdenominational cooperation is Roger Finke and Rodney Stark, *The Churching of America: 1776–1990* (New Brunswick, N.J.: Rutgers University Press, 1992), chapter 6.
8. For one example of contemporary interchurch cooperation, see Lyle E. Schaller, *Center City Churches* (Nashville: Abingdon Press, 1993), pp. 127-37.

4. Seven Forks in the Road into the Third Millennium

1. This strategy is described in greater detail in Lyle E. Schaller, *Innovations in Ministry* (Nashville: Abingdon Press, 1994), chapter 7.

2. Robert Wuthnow, *Christianity in the Twenty-First Century* (New York: Oxford University Press, 1993), p. 134.

3. Ibid., p. 167.

4. Theodore Levitt, *Innovations in Marketing* (New York: McGraw-Hill 1962).

5. 44 Scenarios for Tomorrow

1. Life expectancy projections can be found in The Vital Statistics of the *Statistical Abstract of the United States*, published annually by the United States Bureau of the Census.

2. For an elaboration of the point that participatory democracy often leads to a commitment to the status quo, see Clark Kerr, *The Uses of the University* (Cambridge, Mass.: Harvard University Press, 1982), pp. 176-78.

3. The desire of church members to be heard and understood is described in Robert C. Randall, *What People Expect from Church* (Nashville: Abingdon Press, 1992), pp. 25-28.

4. This competition-oriented model of planning is drawn from Kenichi Ohmae, *The Mind of the Strategist* (New York: McGraw-Hill, 1982), pp. 91-92.

5. See Lyle E. Schaller, *Strategies for Change* (Nashville: Abingdon Press, 1993), pp. 52-58.

6. An excellent introduction to denial is Walter Kiechel III, "Facing Up to Denial," *Fortune* (October 18, 1993): 163-64.

7. For the classic explanation of the distinction between selling and marketing, see Theodore Levitt, *Innovation in Marketing* (New York: McGraw Hill, 1962).

8. For a longer discussion on this alternative, see Lyle E. Schaller, *Expanding Ministries with Retirees, Seasonal Visitors, and Tourists* (New York: United Church Board for Homeland Ministries, 1987).

9. For congregational leaders interested in carving out a distinctive niche, a useful model to examine is the four-year, church-related, liberal college of the 1960s. Between 1960 and 1995, several dozen closed, a few expanded to become mini-universities, while others elected to redefine their role. One new role, as defined by president Harold R. Wilde of North Central College in Naperville, Illinois, is that of the "comprehensive college." Instead of seeking to compete with wealthy research universities or the elite and well-endowed private liberal arts schools, the comprehensive college expands and strengthens the liberal arts core while concur-

rently adding "applied arts" degree programs in market-oriented business administration and computer science fields. This "both-and" role can be more attractive than "either-or" choices.

A strategy that easily can be adapted to churches is described by Ruth B. Cowan, "Prescription for Small College Turnaround," *Change* (January-February 1993): 31-39.

10. Suggestions on relocation of the meeting place can be found in Lyle E. Schaller, *Choices for Churches* (Nashville: Abingdon Press, 1990), pp. 97-121.

11. See Deborah Cronin et al., *New Visions for Small Membership Churches* (New York: General Board of Global Ministries, The United Methodist Church, 1991).

12. An excellent model of this alternative is described in Lyle E. Schaller, *Innovations in Ministry* (Nashville: Abingdon Press, 1994). See item 22, pp. 29-30.

13. Ibid., chapter 7.

14. Among the many useful resources on bivocational ministries, see John Y. Elliott, *Our Pastor Has an Outside Job* (Valley Forge, Pa.: Judson Press, 1980); Stephen P. Whitten, *An Analysis of Churches with Bivocational Pastors, 1991* (Atlanta: Home Mission Board, Southern Baptist Convention, 1993); Vernon Swenson, *What Can Be Done?* (Lima, Ohio: Fairway Press, 1991); Leonard C. Hornick, "Rationale and Development for a Network for a Bi-Vocational Clergy" (D.Min. diss., McCormick Theological Seminary, 1987; Thomas E. Sykes, *Field of Churches* (Atlanta: Home Mission Board, Southern Baptist Convention, 1989); Royal W. Natzke, "Effective Servants for Small Churches" (D.Min. diss., Fuller Theological Seminary, 1987.

15. For a review of the outcomes of congregational mergers, see Lyle E. Schaller, *Reflections of a Contrarian* (Nashville: Abingdon Press, 1989).

6. What Have We Learned?

1. This point is made by Carl Dudley, *Making the Small Church Effective* (Nashville: Abingdon Press, 1979); Peter J. Surrey, *The Small Town Church* (Abingdon Press, 1981); William H. Willimon and Robert L. Wilson, *Preaching and Worship in the Small Church* (Nashville: Abingdon Press, 1980); Lovett H. Weems, Jr., "Leadership Characteristics of the Small Church," *The Christian Ministry* (November-December 1992): 13-15; Nick Taylor, *Ordinary Miracles: Life in a Small*

Notes

Church (New York: Simon and Schuster, 1993); Garret Keizer, *A Dresser of Sycamore Trees* (New York: Viking Press, 1991); and many, many other authors. An excellent description of life in small town America is Thomas H. Rawls, *Small Places: In Search of a Vanishing America* (Boston: Little Brown 1990).